MW00339620

PORSCHE

NEUSCHWANSTEIN

INTRO

Schon lange denken wir über diese „Reise in die Postkarte" nach. Einmal quer über den Süden Deutschlands. Ein Ritt durch vielfältige Kulturlandschaften, durch Regionen, die sich dramatisch voneinander unterscheiden, obwohl sie direkte Nachbarn sind. Und das auf äußerst kurzer Strecke: 1300 Kilometer dauert es, um den Schwarzwald hinunter zu reiten, zum Bodensee hinüber, um dann am Tegernsee vorbei bis ans südöstliche Ende Bayerns zu gelangen. Nur 1300 bunte, heftige, unterhaltsame Kilometer. Zum Vergleich: Auf den CURVES-Reisen durch die USA oder Asien haben wir Tausende Kilometer zurückgelegt. Und dennoch ist die Fahrt am unteren Ende Deutschlands genauso episch und emotional wie die besten Reisen in fernen Ländern. Es liegt an der turbulenten Geschichte dieses Winkels der Welt, am überbordenden Reichtum von Erlebnis und Wandel. Dass Süddeutschland Material für eine überaus faszinierende „Grand Tour" ist, haben wir schon lange geahnt – der erbrachte Beweis liegt viele Seiten stark vor Ihnen. Bilder und Eindrücke hochverdichteter Reiselust. Soulful Driving – auf Deutsch heißt das einfach: „Gute Fahrt."

—

This "journey into a postcard" has been on our wish list for a long time. Once straight across Southern Germany. A ride through diverse cultural landscapes, through regions that, despite being next-door neighbors, are dramatically different. And over such a short distance: it takes just 1300 kilometers to drive through the Black Forest, over to Lake Constance, past Lake Tegernsee to the southeastern end of Bavaria. Just 1300 colorful, powerful, entertaining kilometers. As a comparison, the CURVES trips through the USA or Asia covered thousands of kilometers. And yet the journey at the bottom of Germany is as epic and emotional as the best trips to distant shores. It's because of the turbulent history of this corner of the world, the exuberant wealth of experience and change. We have long suspected that Southern Germany is good terrain for an extremely fascinating Grand Tour – and the following pages are evidence of this. Images and impressions of a highly concentrated wanderlust. We wish you Soulful Driving – have a great trip.

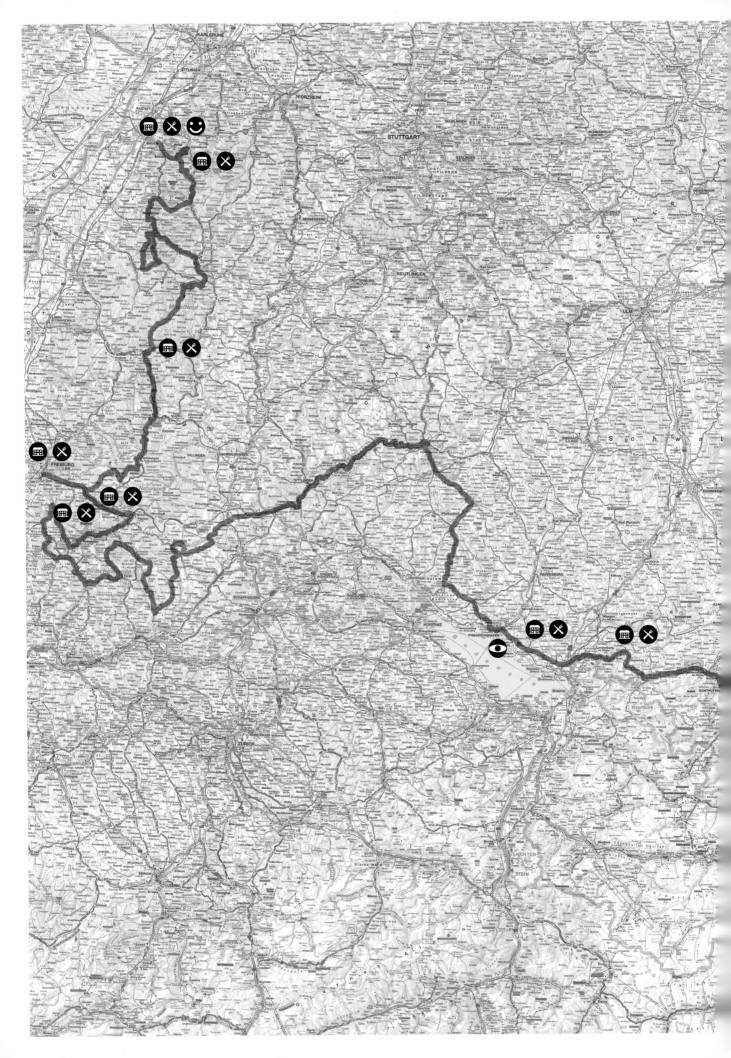

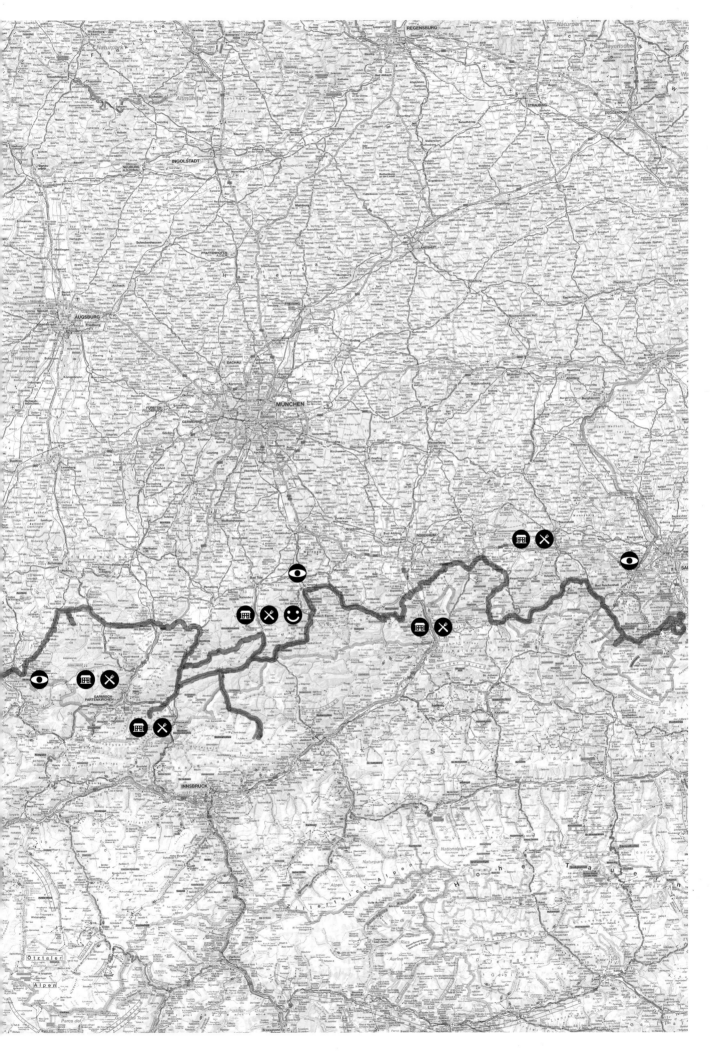

1

2

Rund 200 Kilometer lang zieht sich der Schwarzwald von Nord nach Süd, als erstes großes Hindernis auf dem Weg vom Südwesten Deutschlands in seinen alpinen Südosten. Anstatt ihn aber einfach zu überqueren, entdecken wir ihn beinahe auf ganzer Länge: In der Rheinebene bei Baden-Baden gestartet, werfen wir uns mit Elan auf die kurvigen Straßen des schroffen Nordschwarzwalds und folgen dann der Schwarzwaldhochstraße ins Herz des Mittelgebirges. Zwischen Freudenstadt, Schramberg und Triberg driften wir weit nach Osten ab, entdecken das Land der Bollenhüte und Kuckucksuhren. Der Süden des Schwarzwalds nimmt dann beinahe alpines Format an – auf dem Weg nach Freiburg folgen wir schwingenden Passrouten von Ost nach West.

The Black Forest stretches over almost 200 kilometers from north to south, as the first major obstacle on the way from southwest Germany to its alpine southeast. Instead of simply crossing it, we discover almost all of it: starting in the Rhine Valley near Baden-Baden, we throw ourselves zealously into the twisty roads of the rugged Northern Black Forest then follow the Black Forest High Road into the heart of the low mountain range. Between Freudenstadt, Schramberg and Triberg we drift far to the east, discovering the country of the Bollenhut and cuckoo clock. The south of the Black Forest looks almost alpine-like, on the way to Freiburg we head from east to west over sweeping pass roads.

Der Südschwarzwald hat es verdient, nicht in direkter Linie überquert zu werden, seine Landschaften und Momente sind vielfältig. Das alles sammelt sich in einem überschaubaren Gebiet. Hinzu kommt: Auch wer Fahrfreude sucht, wird hier fündig, die engen und kurvigen Straßen überwinden große Höhenunterschiede und sie sind äußerst abwechslungsreich. Von unserem Ausgangspunkt in Freiburg, der südlichsten Großstadt Deutschlands, fahren wir deshalb zuerst über das Höllental in östlicher Richtung zum Titisee, biegen hier erneut nach Südwesten ab und ziehen über die Feldberg-Region bis Todtnau. Von hier aus geht es zum Schauinsland und damit beinahe wieder nach Freiburg zurück. Auf kurvigen Strecken sind wir nun weiter nach Südosten unterwegs, über das Wiedener Eck und Todtmoss geht es bis nach Sankt Blasien. In einem letzten, weiten Bogen über den Schluchsee, das Schwarza-Schlücht-Tal im Süden und die Wutach-Schlucht am östlichen Rand des Schwarzwalds landen wir im Tal der Donau. Wir begleiten den noch jungen Fluss einige Kilometer und biegen dann nach Süden ab, das Ziel ist der Bodensee.

Southern Black Forest deserves more than being traversed in a straight line, its landscapes and moments are rich, and all within a manageable area. Plus, anyone looking for a delightful excursion will find what they are looking for; the narrow, winding roads cover large altitude differences and are extremely varied. From our starting point in Freiburg, Germany's southernmost city, we first cross the Höllental valley in an easterly direction to Lake Titisee, veer southwest again and travel across the Feldberg region to Todtnau. From here, we head to Schauinsland and almost back to Freiburg, before continuing over snaking roads to the southeast, across the Wiedener Eck and Todtmoss to Sankt Blasien. In a last wide sweep over the Schluchsee, the Schwarza-Schlücht Valley in the south and the Wutach Gorge on the eastern edge of the Black Forest, we land in the valley of the Danube. We accompany the still-young river for a few kilometers before turning south. Destination: Lake Constance.

3 ETAPPE STAGE

Mit seiner enormen Wasserfläche gilt der Bodensee in Deutschland als das Meer der Schwaben – ein etwas vereinnahmender Titel, wenn man weiß, das sein südliches Ufer in der Schweiz liegt und das östliche Ende bei Bregenz zu Österreich gehört. Und bei unserem Etappenstart in Friedrichshafen lässt sich sowieso kaum verbergen, dass die Bodensee-Region alles andere als provinziell ist: Industrie und Technologie gehören schon seit Menschengedenken in diese Ecke. Es dauert viele Kilometer, bis wir den riesigen See hinter uns gelassen haben und dann über den Bregenzerwald ins liebliche Allgäu vorgestoßen sind. Wir streifen diese bemerkenswerte Gegend weit im Süden, hier geht eine uralte Kulturlandschaft mit ganz eigenem Charakter bereits in alpines Gelände über. Hinter Pfronten sind wir dann in Bayern gelandet und rollen entlang der sich immer höher aufbäumenden Berge weiter nach Osten. Mit dem Schloss Neuschwanstein legen wir einen höchst touristischen Zwischenstopp ein – oder lassen ihn aus und konzentrieren uns auf das reine Fahren. Die schmelzenden Gletscher der letzten Eiszeit haben hier die berühmten Seen Oberbayerns hinterlassen: Mit Forggensee und Walchensee erleben wir nicht nur die größten – entlang der Isar und Weißach geht es dann immer weiter in den Osten, bis wir am Tegernsee das Ende unserer Etappe erreichen.

With its huge expanse of water, Lake Constance in Germany is known as the Swabian Sea – a somewhat possessive title considering its southern shore is in Switzerland and the eastern end at Bregenz belongs to Austria. Yet, at the start of this leg in Friedrichshafen, it is very clear that the Lake Constance region is anything but provincial: industry and technology have been part of this corner for as long as people can remember. It takes many kilometers until we've left the huge lake behind us, and continue on to the Bregenz Forest into the delightful Allgäu. We sweep over this remarkable area far to the south, where an ancient cultural landscape with its own character merges into Alpine terrain. After Pfronten we end up in Bavaria and roll further east along the mountains, which tower higher and higher. Neuschwanstein Castle offers a very touristy stopover – or skip it and enjoy the pure driving experience. The melting glaciers of the last ice age have left the famous lakes of Upper Bavaria here, with Forggensee and Walchensee we experience some of the smaller ones – along the Isar and the Weißach we continue east until we reach the end of this leg at Lake Tegernsee.

4 ETAPPE STAGE

Am südlich der bayerischen Landeshauptstadt München gelegenen Tegernsee angekommen, haben wir uns ins Herzland Oberbayerns vorgearbeitet. Bis ans Ende der Reise stehen uns viele, variantenreiche Kilometer über die nördlichen Alpenausläufer bevor. Wir werden tiefe Täler durchfahren, entlang kalter, klarer Seen und immer wieder über majestätisch gespannte Höhenrücken fahren. Zuerst hinüber zum Schliersee, dann durchs Leitzachtal bis Bayrischzell. Hier trudeln wir auf einer herrlichen Serpentinenstrecke aufs Sudelfeld hinauf und genießen die Ausblicke in die umliegende Bergwelt, das sinnliche und gelassene Fahren. Gleich im Anschluss geht es über die Tatzelwurmstraße nach Norden, durchs Inntal und so beinahe in direkter Richtung auf den Chiemsee zu, dem sogenannten Bayerischen Meer. Ein Besuch der berühmten Klosterinseln im See kostet einen ganzen Tag, wer diese Zeit investieren kann, sollte sie sich auf jeden Fall nehmen. Danach nehmen wir in einer südlichen Umschlingung und danach Durchquerung die Chiemgauer Alpen, landen hinter Ruhpolding und Innzell im Berchtesgadener Land. Mit der Panoramastraße am Rossfeld lassen wir die letzte Etappe unserer Reise ausklingen, ein würdiger Höhepunkt.

When we arrived in Tegernsee to the south of the Bavarian capital Munich, we worked our way into the heartland of Upper Bavaria. Before reaching our destination, we have many, varied kilometers ahead of us in the northern foothills of the Alps. We will drive through deep valleys, along cold, clear lakes and again and again over majestic ridges. First over to Schliersee, then through Leitzachtal to Bayrischzell. Here, we meander on a glorious snaking road up the Sudelfeld and enjoy the view of the surrounding mountains and the sensual, relaxed drive. We veer north onto the Tatzelwurm road, through the Inn Valley and almost in a straight line to Chiemsee, the so-called Bavarian Sea. A visit to the famous monastery island in the lake takes a whole day – a must-do if you have the time. Afterwards, we take a southern loop and cross the Chiemgau Alps, and after Ruhpolding and Innzell we end up in Berchtesgadener Land. With the panoramic road at Rossfeld we let the last stage of our trip roll by, a worthy highlight.

SÜDSCHWARZWALD

EDITORIAL

Süddeutschland, das gibt es überhaupt nicht. Nicht als zusammenhängende Landschaft. Nicht als Einheit. Zu sehr zerrten die einstigen europäischen Großmächte über die Badener, Schwaben und Bayern hinweg, als dass man Zeit gehabt hätte, sich zusammenzuraufen. Oder gar eine gemeinsame Identität auszuknobeln. Wer quer durchs Land unterwegs ist, wird verblüfft sein über die manifesten Unterschiede. Sprache und Kultur, Essen und Religion, Temperamente und Wertekataloge sind äußerst vielfältig. Die ehemals kleinen Fürstentümer, die den Südwesten Deutschlands zu einem unüberschaubaren Flickenteppich machten – sie sind immer noch präsent. Das von Adeligen vererbte und vom Klerus verschacherte Land Badens und Württembergs ist kleinteilig, es gibt keine klare, große Geschichte, nur sehr viele kleine Geschichten. Ganz anders verhält es sich beim bayerischen Südosten, der historisch in einer Hand war und dem man dies auch heute noch durch eine durchgehende Grundstimmung abspürt. – All das macht Süddeutschland ungemein reizvoll und spannend. Wer hier mit offenen Augen unterwegs ist, stolpert über dicht gepackte Vergangenheit, und er hat es mit einem Menschenschlag zu tun, der ein Spiegelbild dieser turbulenten und bewegten Geschichte ist.

Vielleicht muss man aus dem Süden Deutschlands kommen, um unter der herzhaften, herben Schale den gutmütigen und zugewandten Kern seiner Leute zu erkennen. Touristen aus dem Ausland verdienen freilich einen vorsichtigen Warnhinweis: Asiatische Kulturen beispielsweise, deren Webmuster aus aufwändig inszenierter und ritualisierter Freundlichkeit besteht, könnten von der robusten Gangart des Bayern im Normalmodus schockiert sein oder die herausfordernde Trockenheit und Strenge der Schwaben leicht als Desinteresse, Besserwisserei oder Ablehnung missverstehen. Selbst Norddeutsche – und deren Heimat beginnt aus der bayerischen Perspektive gleich hinter Nürnberg, aus

Southern Germany actually doesn't exist – at least not as one landscape. Not as one unit. The former great powers of Europe clawed at Baden, Swabia and Bavaria so much that the folk didn't have time to rally themselves – or even to figure out a shared identity. Anyone traveling across the country will be amazed at the glaring differences – the extreme diversity of language and culture, cuisine and religion, temperaments and values. The former tiny principalities that made southwestern Germany a confusing patchwork still exist. Inherited from the nobility and bartered away by the clergy, the land of Baden and Württemberg was divvied up into small parcels. There is no one clear story, just a lot of chapters. The situation is completely different in Bavaria's southeast, which was historically under one rule – a mood that still lingers today. All this makes Southern Germany extremely appealing and exciting. If you travel with your eyes wide open, you will stumble across a densely packed past and encounter a kind of people that reflects this turbulent and eventful history.

Perhaps you need to come from Southern Germany to recognize the good-natured, considerate heart under the tough, gruff skin of its people. Tourists from abroad deserve a word of warning: Asian cultures, for instance, whose weaving pattern consists of elaborately staged and ritualized friendliness, may be shocked by the brusque Bavarian ways, or could easily misunderstand the challenging dryness and austerity of the Swabians for disinterest, presumptuousness or rejection. Even the Northern Germans – and as far as the Bavarians are concerned, their homeland begins just north of Nuremberg, and from the perspective of a Baden-Swabian, somewhere near Cologne – have trouble communicating with Germany's southerners. Not only because the Swabian and Bavarian dialects are so far away from High German: silence in the south earns the highest praise, people regard too much

adisch-schwäbischer Wahrnehmung irgend-
o bei Köln – haben so ihre Kommunikations-
robleme mit den Menschen im Süden Deutsch-
nds. Und das nicht nur, weil sich die Dialekte
er Schwaben und Bayern so weit entfernt vom
ochdeutschen eingependelt haben: Schweigen
lt im Süden als ein herzhaftes Lob, man lehnt
lzu viel Entgegenkommen als unangenehme
nterwürfigkeit oder Bevormundung des Ge-
enübers ab und redet gern mit betont karger
Vortwahl. Es sei denn, es geht um Schimpf-
nd Fluchworte der kernigsten Sorte, dann
t das Repertoire des Bayern üppig, bunt und
infallsreich, und auch die Schwaben kombinie-
en gern bandwurmartige Fluch-Ungetüme
u Liebkosungen für Feind oder noch lieber den
esten Freund. Lediglich wenn es ums Essen
nd Trinken geht, hellen sich die Mienen der
ördlichen Nachbarn auf, jetzt kann endlich
eschlemmt werden. Die Küche der Nordländer
t nämlich von verdrießlicher Hausmannskost
eprägt, in Köln bietet man gar ein belegtes
äsebrot als „Halven Hahn" an – derartige
Iungerleidereien sind im Süden der Republik
ndenkbar. In Baden baut man hervorragen-
en Wein an, die Küche ist von französischer
inesse geprägt. Derbe wird es im Schwarzwald,
ier duftet geräucherter Schinken recht kantig,
ie fast kniehohe Kirschtorte täuscht duftig
Sahne-haubend" große Freundlichkeit vor
nd schlägt dann mit harter, rechter Schnaps-
eraden brutal zu. Mit „Kirsche" ist hier nicht
twa die Frucht gemeint, sondern ihr klares,
lkoholisches Destillat – aber das merkst du
rst, wenn es zu spät ist. Ganze Senioren-Bus-
eisegesellschaften sollen es unter dem Fluch
er Kirschtorte nur mit Mühe, Not und häufigen
topps wieder aus dem Schwarzwald hinaus-
eschafft haben –, um ein Jahr später wieder
chicksalhaft zurückzukehren.

chwaben schwelgt dann in Innereien, Soßen
nd den weltbekannten Spätzle, die auf jeden
all handgeschabt sein müssen, das heißt in
albflüssiger Teigform von einem Holzbrett mit
em Messer in kochendes Wasser geschnipst.
s soll bei diesem Handwerk schon über das
ustandekommen von Ehen entschieden
vorden sein, wenn die Schwiegermutter in
pe der geplanten Zukünftigen des Sohnes beim
pätzleschaben über die Schulter geschaut
nd die Konsistenz des Teigs für ebenso un-
enügend wie die Gestalt der Spätzle befunden
atte. Wiedergutmachung war dann nur mit der
erfekten Maultasche möglich, einer Art

Sie spüren es: Wir können es kaum erwarten, endlich mit Ihnen auf die Reise zu gehen, bei Baden-Baden in den Schwarzwald zu ziehen und erst wieder
von dieser großen Route quer durch Deutschland
abzulassen, wenn wir es bis zum Königssee geschafft haben, ans östliche Ende Bayerns.

It's palpable: We can hardly wait to set out on this
journey with you, to travel from Baden-Baden to
the Black Forest and only let go of this great journey across Germany once we have made it to the
Königssee at the eastern end of Bavaria.

courtesy as unpleasant servility or as patroniz-
ing. They prefer to talk emphatically with very
few words: Unless it has to do with swearing
and cursing: then the earthy repertoire of Bavaria is rich, colorful and extremely creative.
The Swabians, too, like to string together many
words into one long curse, like a caress for their
enemies or, even better, for their best friends.
The faces of the northern neighbors brighten
only when it comes to eating and drinking.
Finally, it's time to feast. The cuisine of the
northerners is characterized by dour home-
style cooking. In Cologne they even offer a
cheese bread roll and call it "half a rotisserie
chicken" – such hunger pangs are unthinkable
in the south of the republic. Baden is famous
for its excellent wines, and the cuisine has a
French finesse. Things get more rustic in the
Black Forest. Here, the dry-cured ham radi-
ates an intense, smoky heartiness; the almost
knee-high cherry gateau seduces with its
delicious creamy topping only to throw a brutal
schnapps uppercut. "Cherry" doesn't really
mean fruit here, but a clear, alcoholic distil-
late – you'll only realize this when it's too late.
Entire busloads of seniors are said to have left
the Black Forest with great difficulty, distress
and many stops under the curse of the Black
Forest Gateau – only to return a year later to do
it all again.

Swabians love livers, kidneys, sauces and the
world-famous spaetzle, a gnocchi-like dough
which must be hand-snipped – or in other
words, cut with a knife on a wooden board and
dropped into boiling water. Legend has it that
suitors for marriage were chosen according to

gefüllter Fleisch-Zwiebel-Brötchen-Riesen-Ravioli, die man wahlweise in Brühe oder überbacken verschlingt. Dass die Maultaschen auch „Herrgottsbscheißerle" genannt werden, Gottesbetrüger also, ist ein hübscher Fingerzeig auf die Religiosität des Südens: Während der Fastenzeiten glaubte man die Fleischfüllung im Nudelmantel der Maultasche vor dem Angesicht des Herrn gut verborgen. Aber die frommen Schwaben trugen auch auf andere Weise zur kulinarischen Fortentwicklung bei: Zuhause in Württemberg galt Fresslust als Verschwendung und Sünde. Dass es im badischen Schwarzwald, in Reichweite des schwäbischen Westens heute viele Sterne-Gastronomen gibt, soll der verstohlenen lukullischen Landflucht vieler Schwaben zu den sonst ungeliebten badischen Nachbarn geschuldet sein. In Bayern ist dann alles anders, aber genau so lecker und deftig: Weißwürste baden in süßem Senf, Schweinshaxen knuspern, Knödel dampfen und beim Nachtisch verrät sich der Bayer als Nachbar und Blutsverwandter des Österreichers: Süß, kross, fruchtig, frittiert und voll zuckriger Verderbtheit schlemmt man sich dem Herzstillstand entgegen. Die ganze Zeit ist der Bierpegel angestiegen – vom badischen Wein bis zum bayerischen Gersten- und Hopfenglück ist es ein weiter Weg. Glücklich, wer ihn ganz hinter sich bringen darf und keinen Tropfen auslassen muss. Es sei aber zugegeben, dass das bayerische Bier nicht umsonst Weltruhm genießt: Drall und fruchtig, angenehm herb, fein und rustikal zugleich schießt es für uns jeden Champagner aus den Socken. Genau so vielfältig wie Geschichte, Kultur, Menschen und Gastronomie des Südens sind seine Landschaften: Einen wirklichen Favoriten haben wir nicht, die eigentümliche Herbheit des Schwarzwalds ist uns ebenso lieb wie das milde Land nördlich des Bodensees, die bayerischen Seen und die wilde Schönheit der Bayerischen Alpen.

Sie spüren es: Wir können es kaum erwarten, endlich mit Ihnen auf die Reise zu gehen, bei Baden-Baden in den Schwarzwald zu ziehen und erst wieder von dieser großen Route quer durch Deutschland abzulassen, wenn wir es bis zum Königssee geschafft haben, ans östliche Ende Bayerns. Wir würden uns aber freuen, wenn sich außer einer großen Lust am unbekümmerten Unterwegssein auch eine Freude an den vielen Geschichten dieses Landes entfalten würde. Eines hat uns dieses Land und seine Geschichte nämlich intensiv gelehrt: Freiheit ist ein Privileg, keine Selbstverständlichkeit. Fahren im CURVES-Stil heißt also: Achtsam sein, respektvoll sein. Offen sein. Aber wem sagen wir das. Genau deshalb sind Sie ja hier.

this handcraft – for instance, when a prospective mother-in-law watched as a potential daughter-in-law snipped the dough, and found that neither the consistency nor the shape of the spaetzle was acceptable. Redemption was possible, but only with the perfect maultasche, a kind of giant ravioli filled with meat-onion-bread and devoured either in a broth or as a gratin. The fact that these dumplings are also called "Herrgottsbscheißerle" (Deceivers of God), is a charming hint to the religious inclination of the south: during Lent, the meat-filling in the maultasche ravioli was thought to be well-hidden from the Lord. But the pious Swabians also contributed to the culinary evolution in other ways: At home in Württemberg, gluttony was regarded as a waste and a sin. So, the Swabians made a stealthy exodus across to Baden's Black Forest – resulting in a high density of Michelin star-studded restaurants today.

In Bavaria it's different, but just as delicious and hearty: Weisswurst bathe in sweet mustard, pork knuckles crackle, dumplings steam and for dessert, the Bavarians reveal themselves as the neighbors and blood relatives of Austria: sweet, crisp, fruity, deep-fried and packed with sugar, feasting towards a heart attack. During this time, the beer tide has risen – it is a long way from the wines of Baden to Bavarian barley and hoppy happiness. Happy are they who can cover the distance without spilling a drop. Admittedly, Bavarian beer is world-famous for good reason: full and fruity, pleasantly bitter, refined yet rustic – for us, it blows any champagne out of the water. The landscapes are just as diverse as the history, culture, people and gastronomy of the south; we don't have one true favorite, we like the peculiar ruggedness of the Black Forest as much as we like the mild landscape north of Lake Constance as well as the lakes of Bavaria and the wild beauty of the Bavarian Alps.

It's palpable: We can hardly wait to set out on this journey with you, to travel from Baden-Baden to the Black Forest and only let go of this great journey across Germany once we have made it to the Königssee at the eastern end of Bavaria. It would give us great pleasure if you find delight not only in the carefree traveling but also in the many stories of this land. This country and its history have taught us one thing above all else: freedom is a privilege, not a right. Driving CURVES-style means: be mindful, be respectful. Be open. But who are we to say? That's exactly why you're here.

ROSSFELD
PANORAMASTRASSE

HINTERSEE

SCHWARZWALD-
HOCHSTRASSE

SYLVENSTEINSPEICHER

**WALCHENSEE
KESSELBERG**

ROSSFELD
PANORAMASTRASSE

OBERJOCH

ROSSFELD
PANORAMASTRASSE

TATZELWURM/
SUDELFELD

ENG

SYLVENSTEINSPEICHER

BADEN-BADEN
FREIBURG

80 KM • 6 STUNDEN // 173 MILES • 6 HOURS

Hinter uns liegt der Rhein, vor uns grüne Höhenzüge im Dunst. Beinahe schwarz sehen sie aus. Das Gegenlicht des Morgens lässt nur Konturen, Schemen und Schatten vom großen Mittelgebirge des deutschen Südwestens übrig – dem Schwarzwald. Ein sehr humorloser Name ist das: Silva Nigra, Schwarzer Wald.

—

At our back the Rhine flows, in front of us the hazy, dark green mountain ridges loom. They seem almost black. The early morning sunrays accentuate the contours, silhouettes and shadows of the long, low mountain range in Germany's southwest – the Black Forest. A rather humorless name, the Silva Nigra, Schwarzwald, Black Forest.

HOTELS

ROOMERS HOTEL BADEN-BADEN
LANGE STR. 100
76530 BADEN-BADEN
WWW.ROOMERS-BADENBADEN.COM

Die Römer haben den Gebirgszug so genannt, wenn sie entlang des Rheins nach Norden unterwegs waren, bis Trier an der Mosel, bis Köln oder auch einmal bis ans Ende der Welt. Nach anfänglicher Distanziertheit scheinen die Römer dann aber doch Zuneigung zur Gegend gefasst zu haben, denn zwischen den Mündungen der kleinen Schwarzwaldflüsse Murg und Oos wurde in heißen Quellen ein Wildnis-Wellness-Bereich für durchgefrorene „Zivilisations-Knochen" eingerichtet. So mancher römische Kaiser sagte hier: „Aah!" Und wollte einfach nur noch baden, baden.

Dieses „Baden-Baden" soll Beginn unserer großen Reise durch den Süden Deutschlands sein, gern würden wir jetzt endlich losfahren, aber es geht einfach nicht. Noch nicht. Denn der Schwarzwald ist kein einfacher, unverfänglicher Anfang für eine Reise. Er ist Dreh- und Angelpunkt so vieler Reisen und Geschichten, die in ungeheurer Intensität zu ihm gehören, und ein paar dieser Geschichten tun nun das, was schon immer ihre Art war: Sie hängen sich an uns Reisende und begleiten uns. Wenn wir ein paar hundert Jahre zurückdrehen, hat unsere Reise durch Deutschland einen ganz anderen Start. Denn dieser Anfang am Fuß des Schwarzwalds ist gleichzeitig das Ende einer anderen, uralten Reise: Weit draußen in der Nordsee tauchen Lachse aus der Tiefe des Atlantiks auf und schwimmen nach Hause in den Rhein. Aus Holland kommend wandern die Fische durch das heutige Nordrhein-Westfalen und Rheinland-Pfalz, folgen dem Lauf des großen Flusses immer weiter nach Süden – erst der Rheinfall bei Schaffhausen, an der südlichen Grenze Deutschlands zur Schweiz, ist ein so großes Hindernis für die Fische, dass sie nicht weiterkommen. Unterwegs verschwinden sie, je nach Herkunft, in den Zuflüssen des Rheins. Einer unserer Lachse könnte also aus dem Schwarzwald stammen, aus der Elz, der Kinzig, der Murg oder Alb. Wenn sich die winzigen, frisch geschlüpften Nachkommen der Fische aus dem Schwarzwald dann zurück auf die Reise ins Meer machen, werden sie von Flößern begleitet: Zwischen dem 15. und 19. Jahrhundert wird das Holz des Schwarzwalds in geradezu industriellem Maßstab

A rather humorless name, the Silva Nigra, Schwarzwald, Black Forest. The Romans gave the mountain chain this name as they traveled north along the Rhine to Trier on the Moselle or to Cologne – or perhaps even to the end of the world. After initial hesitancy, the Romans seem to have taken a liking to the area, because between the mouths of the small Black Forest rivers, the Murg and Oos, a wellness spa was created with thermal springs in the wilderness to thaw the frostbitten bones of the civilized. Some Roman Emperors must have let out a deep sigh and thought: Aah! Let us Baden, Baden... bathe, bathe.

This "Baden-Baden" is supposed to be the beginning of our big trip across Germany's south, and we would very much like to start now... but we can't. At least not yet. Because the Black Forest is not an easy, uncontentious place to start a journey. It is a critical junction for so many adventures and stories that have become tightly woven into the fabric of the place, and now some of these stories do what they've always done: they jump aboard and travel with us. If we turn the clocks back a few hundred years, our trip through Germany would have had a very different beginning – this start at the foot of the Schwarzwald is, at the same time, the end of another archaic journey: From far out in the North Sea from the depths of the Atlantic, salmon make their way home up the Rhine. Coming from Holland, the fish migrate through what is now North Rhine-Westfalia and Rhineland-Palatinate, following the course of the great river further and further to the south – only to encounter a major, insurmountable obstacle at the Rhine Falls near Schaffhausen at Germany's southern border with Switzerland. Depending on the birthplace of the fish, they disappear into the tributaries of the Rhine along the way. One of these salmon could very well have come from the Black Forest, from the Elz, the Kinzig, the Murg or the Alb. When the tiny, freshly hatched fry of the Black Forest fish embark on their journey back to the sea, they will be accompanied by raftsmen: Between the 15th and 19th centuries, the trees in the Black Forest were cut down on an almost industrial scale and floated to marketplaces in the Netherlands. Scenes unimaginable today must have unfolded

bgeholzt und bis an die Handelsplätze in
en Niederlanden geflößt. Heute unvor-
tellbare Szenen müssen sich damals abge-
pielt haben: mächtige Tannenstämme,
ie in aus Holz gezimmerten Rinnen stei-
· Berghänge hinunterdonnern. Kleine
äche, die in so genannten Stuben zu tie-
n Teichen aufgestaut werden und in de-
en sich die Stämme sammeln, zu ersten
leinen Flößen zusammengebunden wer-
en. Dann schlagartiges Wasserablassen –
ie tonnenschweren Stämme gischen
uf einer Flutwelle weiter ins Tal, bis zum
ächstgrößeren Flusslauf und werden von
ort weiter bis zum Rhein geflößt. Mit ent-
panntem Hang-Loose-Surfer-Lifestyle hat
ieser Ritt auf dem Schwall aber nichts
u tun, das Flößen ist eine Blutmühle: Die
chweren Stämme zerschmettern unter-
vegs die Knochen unglücklicher Flößer,
ermalmen Körper.

ı Mannheim, weit nördlich des Schwarz-
ralds, ist der Rhein dann breit und tief
enug, um gewaltige Floßungetüme zu-
ammenzufügen: 600 Meter lang, sechs
Meter hoch und 80 Meter breit. Tausen-
e Stämme machen so ein Floß aus, bis zu
00 Männer steuern das Ungetüm, und
ie haben sich auf dem Deck Unterkünfte
ebaut, Viehställe, Bäckereien und selbst
chlachthäuser. Boote eilen solch einem
Monstrum mit halbtägigem Vorsprung
oraus, um die Dörfer entlang des Fluss-
aufs vor dem unaufhaltsam mit der Strö-
nung den Rhein hinunterdrängenden
ngetüm zu warnen. Um diesen Riesen
us Holz durch die damals noch zahllosen
lusschleifen zu zwingen, sind die Flößer
ag und Nacht in echter Knochenarbeit
eschäftigt – wenn dann die Stämme und
as im Zwischenraum zwischen Boden-
ıge und Decklage mitgeführte Bau- und
rennholz nach wochenlanger Schinde-
ei in den Niederlanden endlich verkauft
verden können, sind nicht wenige Män-
er vor Schuften zerbrochen. Viele aber
teinreich. Das Holz des Schwarzwalds ist
amals sein Gold, die Flößer tragen stattli-
hen Lohn nach Hause, und die Waldbesit-
er sind regelrechte Magnaten in diesem
onst so bitterarmen Landstrich mit sei-
en steilen, kargen Böden und den langen
Vintern. Die bis zu 200 Jahre alten Tan-
en – im Schwarzwald nennt man sie „Hol-
änder" – fahren als Schiffsmasten um die

back then; mighty conifer trunks thundering down steep mountain slopes in wood-
lined chutes. Small streams, dammed into
deep ponds to serve as "holding rooms" for
the trunks, where they are then tied together to form the first small rafts. Then,
the plug is pulled and the trunks, weighing
several tons, are sluiced in the floodwaters
further down the valley and, from there,
floated to the Rhine. This riding of the
wave, however, has nothing to do with the
relaxed hang-loose surfer lifestyle. Rafting
is a bloody business: Heavy logs crush the
bones of unfortunate raftsmen, mashing
bodies along the way.

In Mannheim, in the far north of the
Black Forest, the Rhine flows wide and
deep enough to lash monster rafts together: 600 meters long, six meters high and
80 meters wide. Thousands of trunks for
each raft, needing up to 500 men to tame
the monster, with accommodation on the
deck, cattle stalls, bakeries and even ab-
attoirs. With a half-day lead, boats scuttle
head of the monstrosities, warning villagers downstream of the unstoppable behe-
moth that is being washed down by the
current. To navigate such wooden giants
through the then countless twists and
bends of the Rhine, raftsmen slog day and
night – and by the time the logs, as well as
the building timber and firewood stored
between the lower and upper decks, are finally sold in the Netherlands after weeks
of back-breaking work, more than a few
men are broken. And more than a few have
become extremely rich. The wood from the
Black Forest at that time is gold, the raftsmen bring home a handsome wage, and
the forest owners become magnates in this
otherwise desperately poor stretch of land
with its steep slopes, barren soils and long
winters.

The up to 200-year-old conifers (called
"Dutchmen" in the Black Forest) sail the
oceans of the world as masts and, until
today, serve as piles for houses in the sandy,
damp ground of Rotterdam and Amster-
dam. One could say: The Black Forest begins
at the sea. Our tiny salmon, however,
continue to swim on undisturbed and disappear into the vastness of the Atlantic.
But that's all history now. The Rhine,
once the most important salmon river in

HOTEL / RESTAURANT

WALDHOTEL FORELLENHOF
GAISBACH 91
76534 BADEN-BADEN
WWW.FORELLENHOF-BADEN-BADEN.COM

ROTE LACHE

ROTE LACHE

ROTE LACHE

HUNDSBACH

Velt. Die Häuser Rotterdams und Amsterams stehen heute noch auf Fundamenten us in den sumpfigen Boden gerammten chwarzwaldtannen. Man könnte also saen: Der Schwarzwald beginnt am Meer. Unsere kleinen Lachse schwimmen aber ngerührt weiter und verschwinden in en Weiten des Atlantiks. Das alles ist ber längst vorbei. Der Rhein, einst beeutendster Lachsfluss Europas, ist keine Heimat für die wandernden Fische mehr. Industrie und Abwässer, unvorstellbare egradigungen und gigantische Stauwehe haben die jahrtausendealten Lebensliien abgeschnitten und den ursprünglichen Rhein gebrochen. Heute ist er ein gezähmer Fluss, langsam wird er wieder zum Leensraum – aber die alten, geschuppten Wanderer aus dem Atlantik sind nie wirkich zurückgekehrt. Geflößt wird ebenfalls angst nicht mehr, der ausgebeutete Wald at sich erholen können und die Menchen der Gegend wissen nur noch vom Hörensagen von der grausamen, unerbittichen und glorreichen Arbeit ihrer Vorahren. Oder gar nicht.

Auch wenn von den glamourösen Tagen Baden-Badens als Sommerfrische des euroäischen Jetsets und Adels nicht mehr viel übrig geblieben ist, strahlt die Kurstadt immer noch eine mondäne „Alt-Weltigeit" aus, als wäre die Zeit ein wenig steen geblieben. Als müsste jeden Moment ine Kutsche mit kokett behüteten Damen ms Eck biegen. Als würden die Grand Hoels immer noch auf Gäste in stampfenen Luxus-Cabriolets warten. Als wären Kurhaus, Festspielhaus und Casino immer noch im wiegenden Walzer-Rhythmus unerwegs, auf ewig gefangen beim Tanztee. Baden-Baden hat die zerbrechliche Aura iner alten Dame, wie eine Ahnung von Rosenduft, träumend vom Handkuss des Kavaliers. Spätestens in den Außenbezirken der Stadt ist dieses Gefühl aber verweht. Es bleiben alte Häuserzeilen, die sich chweigend und geraniengrüßend entlang der Oos drängen, während der Fluss in seinem gemauerten Bett in Richtung Rheintal gurgelt. Die Straße folgt dem Tal durch die ähen Ausläufer der Stadt und ihrer Vorrte, immer weiter, und dann irgendvann ist sie frei. Schüttelt die letzten Häuer in ein paar Kehren ab und landet am Forellenhof. Hier strebt die alte Poststraße

Europe, is no longer home to these migratory fish. Industry and effluent, inconceivable engineering of the river course and gigantic weirs have cut the millennia-old lifelines and destroyed the original Rhine. Today, it is a tamed river. Slowly it is becoming a habitat again – but the old, scaled migrants from the Atlantic have never really returned. Rafting also disappeared long ago, the ravaged forests have recovered and the people in the area know of the brutal, relentless, glorious work of their ancestors only from hearsay. Or not at all.

Even if there is not much left of Baden-Baden's golden days as the summer retreat of the European jet-set and nobility, the spa town still exudes a chic, old-world feeling, as if time has stood still. As if a carriage filled with women wearing coquettish hats would swing around the corner at any moment. As if the Grand Hotels were still waiting for guests to arrive in their lurching luxury cabriolets. As if the Spahaus, Festspielhaus and Casino were still swaying to the rhythm of the waltz, forever caught in a tea dance. Baden-Baden has the fragile aura of an elderly lady, like a hint of rose fragrance, dreaming of a hand-kiss from a cavalier. On the outskirts of the city, this feeling fades. Here, rows of old houses, silent and dripping geraniums, huddle along the Oos, while the river bounces along its rock-walled bed towards the Rhine Valley.

The road continues along the valley through tenacious suburbia until at some point it finally breaks free; shaking off the last houses with a few hairpins and end-ing at a trout farm. Here, the old post road from Murgtal in the northeast joins up and we're told that the loop over several kilometers is worth the detour for southbound travelers. As a warm-up, so to speak. So we take a left, fly up the mountain, left, right, left, right, and the following junction is definitely not a matter of opinion: Connoisseurs drive straight on, snake through the dense forest, shift down two gears where the monument to the road builders of the 18th century stands, take the kink with crisp efficiency and land victoriously a couple of kilometers further on at Eberstein Castle. Here, the earth's magnetic field has a mysterious buckle – everyone stops, no matter

HOTEL & RESTAURANT

HOTEL HIRSCHEN
SCHWARZWALDSTRASSE 2-3
77709 OBERWOLFACH
WWW.HOTEL-HIRSCHEN-OBERWOLFACH.DE

aus dem Murgtal im Nordosten kommend herüber, und man hat uns gesagt, die wenige Kilometer lange Runde sei dem nach Süden strebenden Fahrer eine Ablenkung wert. Zum Warmfahren sozusagen. Also links ab, den Berg hinauf fliegen, links, rechts, links, rechts, und der folgende Abzweig ist ganz und gar keine Ansichtssache: Kenner fahren geradeaus, kurven durch den dichten Wald, schalten am Denkmal für die Straßenbaumeister des 18. Jahrhunderts zweimal herunter, nehmen den Knick mit knackigem Pressing und landen ein paar Kilometer weiter glorreich am Schloss Eberstein. Hier hat das Erdmagnetfeld eine mysteriöse Delle – jeder stoppt, egal ob Fahrrad, Motorrad oder Sportwagen. Niemand schafft es, nicht anzuhalten, die Beine von der Mauer am Parkplatz baumeln zu lassen und den magischen Rundumblick die Weinberge hinunter ins Murgtal zu genießen. Für die wenigen herzlosen Schurken, die eine Weiterfahrt ohne Panoramablick planen, hält das Karma des Schwarzwalds böse zuschnappende Schicksalsschläge bereit: Fahrradketten springen, Motorradzündkerzen verrußen und Autobatterie-Massekabel fallen heimtückisch ab. Genau hier hat der Schwarzwald einen ersten Herrder-Ringe-Moment: Du kommst nicht vorbei!

Seelisch eingerenkt und mit öligen Fingern rollen wir dann in geläutertem Trab den Berg hinunter, landen im pittoresken Zentrum des Städtchens Gernsbach und biegen gleich wieder nach links ab, zurück zum Ausgangspunkt. Zuerst gerade den Berg hinauf, dann folgen ein paar versammelt groovende Kurven und schon sind wir zurück. Warmgefahren, geläutert, bereit. Bereit für die „Rote Lache", einem wahren Kurventeufel, dessen Name von den Müttern motorbegeisterter Söhne der Umgebung nur mit Griff zum Rosenkranz und flüsternd ausgesprochen wird. Dass die „Rote Lache" nach heftiger Kurven-Ekstase direkt am Forbacher Krankenhaus landet, war zu den Sturm-und-Drang-Zeiten japanischer Vierzylinder-Motorräder, als die Motoren noch stark und die Fahrwerke schwach waren, vermutlich eine ebenso gefürchtete wie praktische Tatsache. Heute hat sich das wilde Treiben beruhigt, die Vollgas-Helden von einst sind grauhaarig und weise geworden. Wir rollen mit maßvollem Schwung nach Süden, freudig erregt, aber hochkonzentriert und schaffen es so – ganz ohne Probleme – vorüber an der Forbacher Klinik. Für ein paar wenige Kilometer lassen wir es danach auf der Bundestraße 462 ruhig angehen, dann schnappen wir unterhalb der Schwarzenbach-Talsperre wieder nach Kurven. Zwischen Mehliskopf und Unterstmatt haben wir die B 500 erreicht. Als Schwarzwaldhochstraße surft sie in bester Aussichtslage über die Schwarzwaldgipfel und serviert einem immer wieder unfassbare Ausblicke hinunter ins Rheintal. Vorbei an der Hornisgrinde, dem höchsten Berg des Nordschwarzwalds, vorbei an Mummelsee und Seibelseckle bis zum Ruhestein. Oben auf der Höhe ist der Schwarzwald sonnig und offen, Libellen zucken

whether on pushbikes, motorbikes or in sports cars. Nobody manages not to stop, to let their legs dangle from the wall at the parking lot and enjoy the majestic panoramic view down to the vineyards in the Murgtal valley. For the few callous-hearted scoundrels who plan to continue their journey without taking in the panorama, the karma of the Black Forest has some bad strokes of fate in store: bicycle chains break, motorbike spark plugs gather soot and car battery earth cables mysteriously fall off. At this very point, the Black Forest presents one of the first Lord of the Rings moments: there is no way around it! Exhaling a big sigh of relief and with oily hands, we roll down the mountainside at a renovated canter to land in the picturesque town center of Gernsbach, before taking an immediate left and heading back to where we started. First, straight up the mountain, followed by a couple of sweeping curves and we're back. Warmed up, cleansed, ready. Ready for the "Rote Lache", a veritable devil of a corner combination, the name of which is spoken only in hushed tones by local rosary-clutching mothers of car-crazy sons.

The fact the "Rote Lache" ends at the Forbach Hospital after a wild ecstasy of corners very likely serves as both a warning and a convenience during 'Sturm and Drang' era of Japanese four-cylinder motorbikes; when the engines were strong and the chassis were weak. Today, the frenzied times have abated, and the speed fiends of bygone days have become gray-haired and wise. We roll to the south at the measured clip, elated but fully concentrated, and make it past the Forbach Hospital unscathed. For several kilometers we slow the pace along the federal road 462 before swooping into more corners below the Schwarzenbach Dam. Between Mehliskopf and Unterstmatt we reach the B 500, the Black Forest High Road, which surfs along a stunning panoramic crest over the Black Forest peaks, offering incredible vistas down into the Rhine Valley. Past the Hornisgrinde, the highest mountain in the Northern Black Forest, past the Mummelsee lake and Seibelseckle to Ruhestein.

At the top, the Black Forest is sunny and open. Dragonflies flit through moors, grouses hide from the red list of endangered species, while the wolves return and are anything but in the mood for extinction – and we make a second detour that leads us down to the shady halfway slopes and damp valleys. On the lookout for curves. From Ruhestein to the ramshackle All Saints' Abbey, along the Lierbac river almost down to Oppenau, only to make a hasty retreat back into the greenery of the Silva Nigra. At the "Zuflucht", we rejoin the Black Forest High Road and follow it north to close the loop at Ruhestein. Right now would be a good time to loosen the seatbelt, open the windows and recline the seat a little: we now relinquish the wild, rough curves of the Northern Black Forest, change down a gear from the panting, hunting

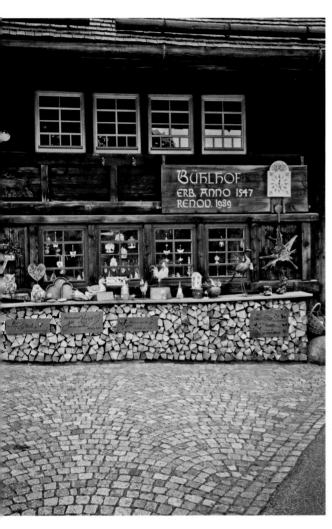

urch Moore, Auerhähne verstecken sich
or der Roten Liste aussterbender Tierar-
en während die Wölfe zurück und alles
ndere als zum Aussterben aufgelegt sind –
nd wir haben einen zweiten Abstecher
or, der uns hinunter in die schattigen
Ialbhöhen und feuchten Täler führt. Auf
er Suche nach Kurven. Vom Ruhestein
um verfallenen Kloster Allerheiligen, ent-
ang des Lierbachs bis beinahe hinunter
ach Oppenau, dann aber schleunigst wie-
er zurück ins grüne Unterholz des Silva
Iigra. An der „Zuflucht" sind wir zurück
uf der Schwarzwaldhochstraße und fol-
en ihr nach Norden, um die Runde am
uhestein zu schließen.

enau jetzt wäre ein guter Moment, um
en Gurt weiter zu ziehen, die Seiten-
cheiben zu öffnen und die Sitzlehne et-
vas flacher zu stellen: Wir lassen nun ab
on den wilden, herben Kurven des Nord-
chwarzwalds, wechseln vom hecheln-
en Jagd-Rhythmus auf den Ruhepuls der
rand Tour. Wir machen uns auf die lange
.eise nach Süden. Im Meer des Schwarz-
valds, während über den Wipfeln Wind-
äder in Zeitlupe furchen, die Mammut-
äume des 21. Jahrhunderts. Die Straße
st eine schnurgerade Schneise im Wald,
ann wieder weite Kurven und Kehren,
vie mit Zirkel und Lineal gezogen. Zuerst
inunter nach Baiersbronn und Freuden-
tadt, dann mit sanft angezogenem Tem-
o bis Bad Rippoldsau und weiter bis ins
inzigtal. Schiltach, dann Schramberg –
ier haben wir den Schwarzwald beinahe
chon bis an seinen östlichen Rand über-
uert. Schnell zurück über die geschwun-
enen Rampen nach St. Georgen und Tri-
erg. Denn der Schwarzwald hat noch so
iel zu erzählen.

Vährend wir über Furtwangen und St. Mär-
en nach Südwesten in Richtung Kirch-
arten und Freiburg streifen, laufen in uns
ilder und Eindrücke randvoll. Gestern noch
achten wir, dieser Schwarzwald sei nur
ine erste notwendige Etappe auf dem Weg
inüber zu den sonnigen Alpen Deutsch-
ands. Eine Straße zwischen Bäumen, ein
nspektakuläres und müdes Land. Jetzt
vissen wir: Tiefer, härter und knorriger kann
ine Reise nicht beginnen.

Genau jetzt wäre ein guter Moment, um den Gurt weiter zu ziehen, die Seitenscheiben zu öffnen und die Sitzlehne etwas flacher zu stellen: Wir lassen nun ab von den wilden, herben Kurven des Nordschwarzwalds, wechseln vom hechelnden Jagd-Rhythmus auf den Ruhepuls der Grand Tour. Wir machen uns auf die lange Reise nach Süden.

Right now would be a good time to loosen the seatbelt, open the windows and recline the seat a little: we now relinquish the wild, rough curves of the Northern Black Forest, change down a gear from the panting, hunting rhythm to the resting pulse of the Grand Tour. We set out on the long stint to the south.

rhythm to the resting pulse of the Grand Tour. We set out on the long stint to the south. Through the ocean of forest, while above the treetops the wind turbines – sequoias of the 21st century – gyrate in slow motion. The road slices through the forest in a straight line, then sweeping curves and hairpin bends as if drawn by a compass and ruler. First down to Baiersbronn and Freudenstadt, at a flowing clip to Bad Rippoldsau and on to the Kinzig valley. Schiltach then Schramberg – at this point we have almost reached the eastern border of the Black Forest. We quickly scamper back up the snaking slopes to St. Georgen and Triberg. After all, the Black Forest has so much to tell.

As we trek southwest over Furtwangen and St. Märgen towards Kirchzarten and Freiburg, our heads are bursting with images and impressions. Yesterday we thought that this Black Forest was simply the first unavoidable leg on the way to the sunny German Alps. A road between trees, an unspectacular and weary land. Now we know: No journey can begin deeper, harder and gnarlier than this.

HOTELS / RESTAURANTS

TRESCHERS SCHWARZWALD
ROMANTIKHOTEL SEESTRASSE 10
79822 TITISEE-NEUSTADT
WWW.SCHWARZWALDHOTEL-TRESCHER.DE

HOTEL RAINHOF SCHEUNE
HÖLLENTALSTRASSE 96
79199 KIRCHZARTEN-BURG
WWW.RAINHOF-HOTEL.DE
WWW.PRETTY-HOTELS.COM

DESIGNHOTEL AM STADTGARTEN
KARLSTRASSE 12
79104 FREIBURG IM BREISGAU
WWW.HOTELAMSTADTGARTEN.DE

BADEN-BADEN FREIBURG

Rund 200 Kilometer lang zieht sich der Schwarzwald von Nord nach Süd, als erstes großes Hindernis auf dem Weg vom Südwesten Deutschlands in seinen alpinen Südosten. Anstatt ihn aber einfach zu überqueren, entdecken wir ihn beinahe auf ganzer Länge: In der Rheinebene bei Baden-Baden gestartet, werfen wir uns mit Elan auf die kurvigen Straßen des schroffen Nordschwarzwalds und folgen dann der Schwarzwaldhochstraße ins Herz des Mittelgebirges. Zwischen Freudenstadt, Schramberg und Triberg driften wir weit nach Osten ab, entdecken das Land der Bollenhüte und Kuckucksuhren. Der Süden des Schwarzwalds nimmt dann beinahe alpines Format an – auf dem Weg nach Freiburg folgen wir schwingenden Passrouten von Ost nach West.

—

The Black Forest stretches over almost 200 kilometers from north to south, as the first major obstacle on the way from southwest Germany to its alpine southeast. Instead of simply crossing it, we discover almost all of it: starting in the Rhine Valley near Baden-Baden, we throw ourselves zealously into the twisty roads of the rugged Northern Black Forest then follow the Black Forest High Road into the heart of the low mountain range. Between Freudenstadt, Schramberg and Triberg we drift far to the east, discovering the country of the Bollenhut and cuckoo clock. The south of the Black Forest looks almost alpine-like, on the way to Freiburg we head from east to west over sweeping pass roads.

280 KM • 6 STUNDEN // 173 MILES • 6 HOURS

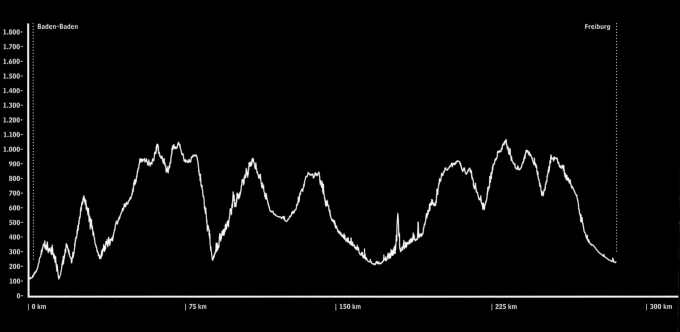

FREIBURG FRIEDRICHS-HAFEN

385 KM • 7 STUNDEN // 239 MILES • 7 HOURS

Hier wollten sie alle hinüber: Die Händler, die Reisenden und die Heere. Aus dem Westen kommend, aus dem Elsass, Lothringen oder der Champagne, und dann am sonnigen Freiburg vorbei aufs Hochplateau des Schwarzwalds und weiter in den Osten, wo sich die Welt zu den Alpen hin öffnet und man bereits wagt, an Italien zu denken. Aber erst einmal musste man durch die Ravennaschlucht und das Höllental.

—

They all wanted to pass through here: the traders, the travelers, the armies. From the west, from Alsace, Lorraine or Champagne, and then past sunny Freiburg to the high plateau of the Black Forest and further east, where the world opens up to the Alps and you dare to think about Italy. But first, one must endure the Ravenna Gorge and Höllental (Hell's Valley).

RAVENNASCHLUCHT

HOTEL

DIE HALDE
HALDE 2
79254 OBERRIED
WWW.HALDE.COM

Die Bundesstraße 31 hat es sich heute auf der alten Handelsstraßen-Trasse über den Schwarzwald eingerichtet. Sie zieht geradewegs nach Osten und das so lange, bis links und rechts der Route steile Felswände enger rücken und die Straße in den Schwitzkasten nehmen. Die wehrt sich, windet sich, wütet mit drei Fahrspuren gegen diesen Zangengriff an und muss am Ende doch klein beigeben: Kräftige Serpentinen und enge Kehren über drei, vier, fünf Stockwerke sind notwendig, bis sich die B 31 nach oben in den Trichter des Höllentals gekämpft hat. Die Welt öffnet sich jetzt, Wiesen, Hügel und grüne Matten liegen im Sonnenlicht, von hier aus breitet sich der Schwarzwald als sanft gewölbtes Plateau nach Osten aus. Geschafft.

Wir folgen der nun mit neuem Schwung nach Osten strebenden Bundesstraße 31 aber nur noch für wenige Kilometer, am Titisee begegnen wir einer alten Bekannten: Die den Nordschwarzwald als Schwarzwaldhochstraße durchschneidende B 500 haben wir gestern bei Furtwangen verlassen, folgen nun ein weiteres Mal für knapp 10 Kilometer ihrem Lauf und biegen dann nach Westen ab. Vor uns liegt jetzt der 1493 Meter

The federal highway 31 has replaced the old trade route over the Black Forest. It heads due east until steep rock faces close in on the left and right and grab the road in a stranglehold. With its three lanes, it resists, writhes and rages against the pincer grip and ultimately has to surrender: the #31 follows powerful switchbacks and tight hairpins over three, four, five stories to the top until it struggles its way into the funnel of the Höllental. The world now opens up, meadows and hills and green carpets bathe in the sunlight, from here the Black Forest spreads out to the east as a gently curving plateau. We made it.

We now follow the federal highway 31 as it unfolds to the east, but only for a few kilometers. At Lake Titisee we meet up with an old acquaintance: yesterday, we'd left the B500 Black Forest High Road at Furtwangen, which cuts through the Northern Black Forest, and now we rejoin it for almost 10 kilometers and turn to the west. Ahead of us stands the 1,493-meter-high Feldberg, Germany's highest peak outside the Alps. Up here, the Southern Black Forest shows its true nature, its rocky foundation. Above the dense, green forest, a treeless crown stands

hohe Feldberg, Deutschlands höchster Gipfel außerhalb der Alpen. Hier oben zeigt der Südschwarzwald sein eigentliches Wesen, sein steinernes Grundgerüst. Aus dem dichten, grünen Wald erhebt sich eine baumlose Kuppe mit weiteren Nebenkuppen, die knorrige Namen wie Seebuck oder Baldenweger Buck tragen.

Dicht unterhalb des Feldbergs segeln wir vorbei, haben es nach den Etappen in dichtem Wald jetzt in eine andere Welt geschafft. Still ist sie und einsam, die wenigen Ortschaften sammeln sich in Tälern zwischen den Hügelkuppen. Kleinteilige Waldstücke umschließen wie die Teile eines unfertigen Puzzles sattgrüne Wiesenhänge, kleine Bäche glucksen in tief eingeschnittenen Rinnen, und immer wieder ducken sich die breiten Häuser und Scheunen von Bauernhöfen in die schützenden Winkel dieser Landschaft. Mächtige Dächer haben diese Höfe, ihre Firste und Giebel sind wie riesige Kappen weit über das eigentliche Bauwerk gespannt, um während der langen Winter ausreichenden Schutz gegen Schnee und Wind zu bieten. Dunkle Fenster spähen ins Land, kleine Sträßchen und Feldwege spannen ihr Netz über diese Welt unter einem weiten Himmel. Bei Todtnau biegen wir erneut für einen Abstecher nach Norden zum Notschreipass ab. Jetzt fällt es uns zum ersten Mal auf: Die Schwarzwälder scheinen gelegentlich eine äußerst zwiespältige Beziehung zu ihrer Heimat zu haben, viele Ortsnamen raunen Bitternis und Desillusion. Hinter Schlechtnau kommt hier gleich Todtnau, und wer auf dem Weg über das Gebirge unter die sonnige, gemütliche Oberfläche schaut, begegnet alten und bösen Geschichten. Dunkle Geister und Dämonen hausen in Felsen, Bäumen und kreisrunden, düsteren Bergseen. Verlorene Seelen hasten über kleine Pfade im Wald und locken Wanderer in Sümpfe und ins Dickicht. Er hat eine wirklich schwarze Seite, dieser Schwarzwald. Und all das hat nichts zu tun mit finsteren Mächten, sondern mit der ehemals bitteren Armut und erschreckenden Wegelosigkeit der Gegend. Die ganze Welt erzählt sich schaudernd das Märchen von Hänsel und Gretel. Dass die Brüder Grimm ihre durchaus reale Vorlage aus dem Schwarzwald haben, dürfte aber den Wenigsten bekannt sein. Es ist keine 500 Jahre her, dass die Menschen des

shoulder to shoulder with smaller peaks bearing gruff names like Seebuck and Baldenweger Buck.

We sail by just below the Feldberg. After the thick woodland, we now find ourselves in another world. It is quiet and reclusive, with hamlets scattered few and far between in the valleys between the hilltops. Small stands of trees enfold lush green meadows, like pieces of an unfinished puzzle; small streams chuckle in deeply-carved watercourses. Every so often, stout houses and barns hunker in the sheltered corners of this landscape. These farmhouses have mighty roofs, their ridges and gables look like huge caps stretched wide over the buildings, providing protection from snow and wind during the bleak winters. Dark windows peek into the countryside, a network of narrow lanes and dirt tracks crisscross over this world under a big sky.

At Todtnau we turn again to take a detour to the north, to the Notschreipass, and now we notice something for the first time: The people of the Black Forest sometimes seem to have an extremely ambivalent relationship towards their homeland; many place names allude to bitterness and disillusionment. Right after Schlechtnau (badlands) comes Todtnau (meadow of the dead), and if you dig under the sunny, cozy surface on the way over the mountains, you will encounter old and evil stories. Dark spirits and demons live in the rocks, trees and perfectly circular, bleak mountain lakes. Lost souls scuttle along narrow forest paths and lure hikers into swamps and thickets. It truly has a dark side, this Black Forest. And all of this has nothing to do with evil forces, but with the bitter poverty and the hopeless remoteness of the area. The whole world shudders as it tells the fairy tale of Hansel and Gretel – but very few realize that the Brothers Grimm took inspiration for the story from the Black Forest. It is not even 500 years ago that the folk of the Black Forest had to abandon their children in the woods in times of starvation – what is shown in such a cold, cynical and banal way in the fairy tale is, in fact, a deeply traumatic chapter in the history of this region. And in other myths, when dwarfs sing as they dig for buried treasures in deep tunnels, we now know the true essence behind this innocent image: children

Schwarzwalds in Hungerzeiten ihre Kinder in den Wald führen mussten. Was im Märchen so kalt, zynisch und banal geschildert wird, ist ein tiefes Trauma dieses Lands. Und wenn in anderen Legenden Zwerge singend in tiefe Stollen ziehen, um nach verborgenen Schätzen zu graben, weiß man heute um den wahren Kern dieses unschuldigen Bilds: Bereits mit sechs oder acht Jahren wurden die Kinder der Gegend in die Silber- und Eisenerz-Stollen geschickt, zogen in der Dunkelheit des Morgens mit ihren Brüdern und Vätern unter Tage und kehrten besonders in den Herbst- und Wintermonaten erst nach Hause zurück, wenn die Sonne längst wieder untergegangen war. Dieses Leben ohne Tageslicht bremste jedes Wachstum des Körpers. Wenn die Bergleute des Schwarzwalds dann völlig abgewirtschaftet in ihren Dreißigern starben, waren sie Zwerge geblieben. Heute klingt das nach vergeudeten Leben – in den Gesellschaften des 17. oder 18. Jahrhunderts wurde das Privileg ein Bergmann zu sein aber hart verteidigt. Es gab weitaus härtere Schicksale und Arten, hier oben sein Dasein zu fristen, im Schwarzwald wurde hart gelebt und früh gestorben. Wir könnten uns also im Süden des Mittelgebirges auch auf eine andere Reise machen, die eines Auswanderers: Nicht wenige Schwarzwälder kehrten ihrer Heimat für immer den Rücken, fuhren mit der Donau nach Osten, um ihr Glück in den Weiten Russlands zu suchen oder traten den Weg nach Westen an. Über den Rhein ans Meer, dann die Überfahrt nach Amerika. Es ist noch nicht so lange her, dass der Schwarzwald immer nur Ausgangspunkt vieler Wanderungen und Reisen war und niemals das Ziel.

Schön, dass nach dem Notschreipass dann der Schauinsland kommt, der 1283 Meter hohe Hausberg Freiburgs. Seinen hübschen Namen trägt dieser enorme Plateauberg vollkommen zu Recht. In alle Richtungen schweift der Blick beinahe ungehindert: Ins Land hinein ziehen sich die bewaldeten Schwarzwaldhügel mit ihren kahlen Kuppen, die Sonne dringt jetzt am späten Morgen aus einem strahlend blauen Himmel bis hinunter in die wilden Täler. Hinter Freiburg dehnt sich das Rheintal bis an den Horizont, in blauem Dunst ist die Bergkette der Vogesen zu erkennen, drüben in Frank-

as young as six were sent down into the silver and iron ore mines, forced underground at dawn to work alongside their brothers and fathers, only to emerge after the sun had set in the months of fall and winter. This life without sunlight stunted their growth. When the miners of the Black Forest died exhausted in their thirties, they were still the size of dwarfs.

Today, this sounds like a wasted life – however, in the societies of the 17th and 18th centuries, the privilege of being a miner was fiercely defended. There were far tougher fates and livelihoods up here; life in the Black Forest was hard, and people died young. So we could take another journey in the south of the low mountain range; one of the emigrant. More than a few folk from the Black Forest turned their backs on their homeland forever. They pushed east on the Danube to seek happiness in the vastness of Russia; or set out to the west, with the Rhine to the sea, then across the pond to America. It was not so long ago that the Black Forest was popular as the starting point for many hikes and trips, but never the destination.

How wonderful it is, then, that straight after the Notschreipass (cry of distress pass) we reach "Schauinsland" mountain (look into the country), Freiburg's own 1,283-meter-high mountain. The charming name of this vast table mountain is befitting: the view sweeps almost unhindered in every direction. The bald-headed wooded hills of the Black Forest rise from the land, the late morning sun in the piercingly blue sky floods into the wild valleys. After Freiburg, the Rhine Valley stretches to the horizon, the mountain range of the Vosges can be seen in the blue haze of distant France. We take a break to catch our breath for the next stage – it's a tough one. Or at least it used to be. While the cabins of the Schauinsland cable car slowly approach the terminal at the summit, we swoosh down the mountain to Horben. Once there, we turn around and, from this point on, a blockbuster movie plays in our minds. Between 1923 and 1989, a famous mountain race was contested on the route up the Schauinsland. In its heyday, it was one of the biggest hill-climb events on the motor racing calendar. Today, the race

ich. Wir legen eine Pause ein. Holen Luft ir die nächste Etappe. Denn die hat es in ch. Oder besser: Hatte. Während die Gon-ln der Schauinslandbahn ihre letzten Hö-nmeter zurücklegen und dann langsam a die Bergstation tauchen, rollen wir den erg hinunter nach Horben. Unten ange-ommen machen wir kehrt, und ab jetzt iielt Kopfkino eine große Rolle. Zwischen 023 und 1984 wurde auf der Strecke zum chauinsland hinauf ein berühmtes Berg-ennen ausgetragen, das während der Hey-ays der europäischen Bergrennen zu den nz Großen im Motorsport-Kalender gehör-. Heute ist das Rennen längst Geschichte, reiburgs Politik fest in grüner Hand und las Schauinsland" temporeguliert. The imes They Are A-Changin', und wir wollen a gar nicht klagen. Manche Dinge haben en ein Verfallsdatum.

ie musikalische Entdeckung ist: Man ann den Berg auch mit langsamem Groove hren, die vollen 180 Beats Per Minute sind icht notwendig –, obwohl man sich in anchen Ecken schon fragt, wie es sich an-ihlen würde, mit einem ausgedrehten Por-che 908 durch die langgezogene Rechtskur-e an der „Holzschlägermatte" zu prügeln. anz außen an den Granitrandsteinen an-hren, mit krampfendem Bizeps und ohne a blinzeln im Scheitelpunkt innen übers ras und dann in den beinahe unsichtbar n dunklen Wald liegenden Kurvenaus-ang hinein. Oder die herrlichen Wechsel-urven ein paar Kilometer vorher: sanfter rift, brutaler Tempoüberschuss über alle ier Räder schiebend runtergedrückt, und ann dieses göttergleiche Gefühl, wenn es it möglichst viel Schwung auf die nächste erade ging. Aber nein, heute schnüren wir nfach genüsslich nach oben, rund 780 Hö-enmeter auf 12 Kilometer verteilt und – eil das Fahren gerade so schön ist, die wil-en Zeiten aber längst vergangen – lassen en Zieleinlauf oben am Schauinsland-Pla-au einfach ausfallen. Schippern stattdes-en an der engen Linkskehre direkt nach er Holzschlägermatte geradeaus. In Rich-ng Obermünstertal, dann über den Pass m Wiedener Eck, und die Strecke schwingt tzt, surft geschmeidig, fließt nur noch so. Ver braucht schon ein Rennen, wenn er die efühlvolle und anhaltendere Variante ha-en kann. Unten in Utzenfeld links ab nach schwend, dann durch den Präger Glet-

is a thing of the past, Freiburg's politics are firmly in green hands and the speed up "the Schauinsland" has been capped. The Times They Are A-Changin'– and we don't want to complain. Some things simply have an ex-piry date.

The musical discovery is that you can drive up the mountain at a relaxed tempo, the full 180 beats per minute are not necessary – al-though, admittedly, in some corners, one wonders how it would feel to hurtle flat-out through the sweeping right-hander at the Holzschlägermatte at the wheel of a red-lin-ing Porsche 908. To drift to the outside of the granite curbs with clenched biceps and, without blinking, take the apex over the grass to then find the exit to the corner, which is almost invisible in the dark forest. Or the wonderful serpentine combination a few kilometers beforehand: a gentle power-slide over all four wheels takes the sting out of the speed, and the heavenly feeling of taking as much momentum as possible with you onto the next straight. But no, today we simply savor the climb over 12 ki-lometers to an altitude of almost 780 meters and, because the driving is so wonderful, we simply forget about those wild times and miss the finish line at the top of the Schau-insland plateau. Instead, we sail straight ahead at the tight left-hander directly after the Holzschlägermatte. Towards Ober-münstertal, then over the pass at the Wie-dener Eck, the road now sways in smooth curls, flowing just so. Who needs a compe-tition when you can have this more soul-ful and prolonged version. Down in Utzen-feld we veer left to Gschwend, then through the Präg glacial basin and after Todtmoos to the east. But we are in no hurry to leave the Feldberg area, a final sweep from Sankt Blasien leads us north, over Menzenschwand to the Schluchsee reservoir lake. In the ear-ly 1930s, the Schwarza River was dammed here around the original Schluchsee, the resulting reservoir then swallowed up the old glacier lake and the surrounding upland moors. From here, we could drive the few ki-lometers to Bonndorf in the east, but before we tackle the eastern foothills of the Black Forest and work our way towards Lake Con-stance, we make a final foray to the south. Along the Schwarza to the south, into the Schlücht valley and only then head back to the north. Down here, close to the Swiss

HOTELS

HOTEL RAD
LINDAUER STRASSE 2
88069 TETTNANG
WWW.HOTEL-RAD.COM

RIVA - DAS HOTEL AM BODENSEE
GOURMETRESTAURANT OPHELIA
SEESTRASSE 25
78464 KONSTANZ
WWW.HOTEL-RIVA.DE

RESTAURANT/SUNDOWNER:
ZUM SANDSEELE 1
78479 INSEL REICHENAU
WWW.SANDSEELE.DE

RESTAURANT SCHUPPEN 13
ARGENWEG 60
88085 LANGENARGEN
WWW.SCHUPPEN13.DE

cherkessel und hinter Todtmoos nach Osten. So schnell
assen wir die Feldberg-Gegend aber noch nicht im Stich,
in letzter Schwung führt uns in Sankt Blasien nach Nor-
en, über Menzenschwand zum Schluchsee. Zu Beginn der
930er-Jahre wurde hier rund um den Ur-Schluchsee die
chwarza aufgestaut. Der dann entstandene heutige Stau-
ee hat den alten Gletschersee und das umgebende Hoch-
moor verschluckt. Von hier aus könnten wir die wenigen
ilometer bis Bonndorf nach Osten fahren, aber bevor wir
ort die östlichen Ausläufer des Schwarzwalds in Angriff
ehmen und uns weiter in Richtung Bodensee vorarbei-
en, haben wir uns einen letzten Abstecher nach Süden
orgenommen. Entlang der Schwarza nach Süden, hi-
ein ins Tal der Schlücht und erst jetzt zurück nach Nor-
en. Hier unten, dicht an der Schweizer Grenze, wird der
chwarzwald mild und das Land legt die Schroffheit der
öhenlagen ab. Sattgrüne Flusstäler schlängeln sich unter
elstürmen dahin – auch die Schlucht der Wutach hinter
onndorf hat diesen üppigen urwaldartigen Charakter.

angsam löst sich der Schwarzwald auf, wir haben seinen
ücken hinter uns gelassen und rollen nun in eine andere
andschaft hinein. Irgendwo auf den letzten Kilometern
at sich aber auch noch ein anderer Wechsel angebahnt:
ie Sprache und vielleicht sogar das Gemüt der Bewoh-
er verändern sich. Ganz grob gesagt wird der badische
Vesten des Schwarzwalds von den Nachfahren des alten
ermanenstamms der Alemannen bestimmt, ihre Kul-
ur und der lebhafte alemannische Dialekt ziehen sich bis
ns Elsass und hinunter in die Schweiz. Während wir nun
ber in Richtung des Donautals rollen, wechseln wir auf
as Gebiet der Schwaben, die Sprache wird härter, sie kaut
ie Silben breit und stark, zieht die Vokale und gurgelt die
onsonanten. Hinter Donaueschingen sind wir endgültig
n alten Württemberg unterwegs, das Land Baden und
er Schwarzwald sind Geschichte. Im Tal der Donau geht
s unter Millionen Jahre alten Kalkriffen dahin, der Fluss
t noch klein und jung, aber man spürt ihm bereits ab,
ie weit es ihn tragen wird: quer durch Deutschland und
sterreich, immer weiter nach Osten, durch insgesamt
ehn Länder Europas, bis er alt und breit und müde ins
chwarze Meer mündet. Bis Sigmaringen folgen wir die-
er Donau im Kindergartenalter, dann zieht es uns in
erader Linie nach Südosten: Krauchenwies, vorbei an
fullendorf, direkt auf den Bodensee zu. Bei Friedrichshafen
ollen wir ans Ufer des „Schwäbischen Meers", diesem über
30 Quadratkilometer großen Überrest der Alpengletscher.
riedrichshafen – das ist nicht nur eine der größten Städte
m Bodensee, sondern auch ein Ort, an dem Luftfahrtge-
chichte geschrieben wurde. Von hier aus fuhren Zeppe-
ne in die Welt, auf dem Spiegel des Bodensees starteten
ächtige Dornier-Wasserflugzeuge. Neuer Stoff für eine
ntdeckungsreise. Die lange Etappe über den Südschwarz-
vald hat das Sitzfleisch beansprucht, alle Konzentration
efordert, und da kommt das Eintauchen in die Welt des
ornier Museums gerade recht.

Hier unten, dicht an der Schweizer Grenze, wird der Schwarzwald mild und das Land legt die Schroffheit der Höhenlagen ab.

Down here, close to the Swiss border, the Black Forest becomes mellow and the countryside casts off the ruggedness of the high altitudes.

border, the Black Forest becomes mellow and the country-side casts off the ruggedness of the high altitudes. Verdant river valleys meander under rock towers – the Wutach Gorge after Bonndorf also has this lush, jungle-like character.

The Black Forest slowly retreats, it is now in our rear-view mirror and we are rolling through another landscape. Somehow, over the last kilometers, another change has occurred: the language and perhaps even the disposition of the people here are different. Broadly speaking, the Baden west of the Black Forest is dominated by the descendants of the old Germanic tribe of the Alemanni, their culture and lively Alemannic dialect reaches as far as Alsace and down to Switzerland. But, as we glide towards the Danube Valley, we find ourselves in Swabia; where the language turns rougher, the syllables chewed, the vowels drawn out and the consonants gargled. After Donaueschingen we finally reach old Württemberg; the state of Baden and the Black Forest are history. In the valley of the Danube, we pass limestone reefs that are millions of years old, the river is still small and young, but you can already sense how far it reaches: right across Germany and Austria, further and further east, through ten European countries, until it flows old and wide and tired into the Black Sea. We follow this kindergarten-aged Danube until Sigmaringen, then head straight to the southeast: Krauchenwies, past Pfullendorf, all the way to Lake Constance. At Friedrichs-hafen, we roll to the shores of the Swabian Sea, a 530-square-kilometer remnant of Alpine glaciers. Friedrichs-hafen is not only one of the largest cities on Lake Constance, but also a place where aviation history was written. From here, the first zeppelins flew into the world, powerful Dornier seaplanes took off on the calm surface of Lake Constance. New content for a journey of discovery. The long leg over the Southern Black Forest has taken staying power and total concentration. Immersing ourselves in the world of the Dornier Museum is just the answer.

MUSEUM

DORNIER MUSEUM
CLAUDE-DORNIER-PLATZ 1
88046 FRIEDRICHSHAFEN
WWW.DORNIERMUSEUM.DE

FREIBURG FRIEDRICHSHAFEN

Der Südschwarzwald hat es verdient, nicht in direkter Linie überquert zu werden, seine Landschaften und Momente sind vielfältig. Das alles sammelt sich in einem überschaubaren Gebiet. Hinzu kommt: Auch wer Fahrfreude sucht, wird hier fündig, die engen und kurvigen Straßen überwinden große Höhenunterschiede und sie sind äußerst abwechslungsreich. Von unserem Ausgangspunkt in Freiburg, der südlichsten Großstadt Deutschlands, fahren wir deshalb zuerst über das Höllental in östlicher Richtung zum Titisee, biegen hier erneut nach Südwesten ab und ziehen über die Feldberg-Region bis Todtnau. Von hier aus geht es zum Schauinsland und damit beinahe wieder nach Freiburg zurück. Auf kurvigen Strecken sind wir nun weiter nach Südosten unterwegs, über das Wiedener Eck und Todtmoss geht es bis nach Sankt Blasien. In einem letzten, weiten Bogen über den Schluchsee, das Schwarza-Schlücht-Tal im Süden und die Wutach-Schlucht am östlichen Rand des Schwarzwalds landen wir im Tal der Donau. Wir begleiten den noch jungen Fluss einige Kilometer und biegen dann nach Süden ab, das Ziel ist der Bodensee.

—

Southern Black Forest deserves more than being traversed in a straight line, its landscapes and moments are rich, and all within a manageable area. Plus, anyone looking for a delightful excursion will find what they are looking for; the narrow, winding roads cover large altitude differences and are extremely varied. From our starting point in Freiburg, Germany's southernmost city, we first cross the Höllental valley in an easterly direction to Lake Titisee, veer southwest again and travel across the Feldberg region to Todtnau. From here, we head to Schauinsland and almost back to Freiburg, before continuing over snaking roads to the southeast, across the Wiedener Eck and Todtmoss to Sankt Blasien. In a last wide sweep over the Schluchsee, the Schwarza-Schlücht Valley in the south and the Wutach Gorge on the eastern edge of the Black Forest, we land in the valley of the Danube. We accompany the still-young river for a few kilometers before turning south. Destination: Lake Constance.

385 KM • 7 STUNDEN // 239 MILES • 7 HOURS

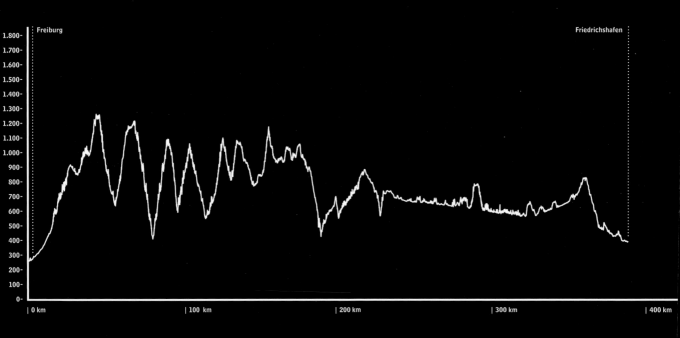

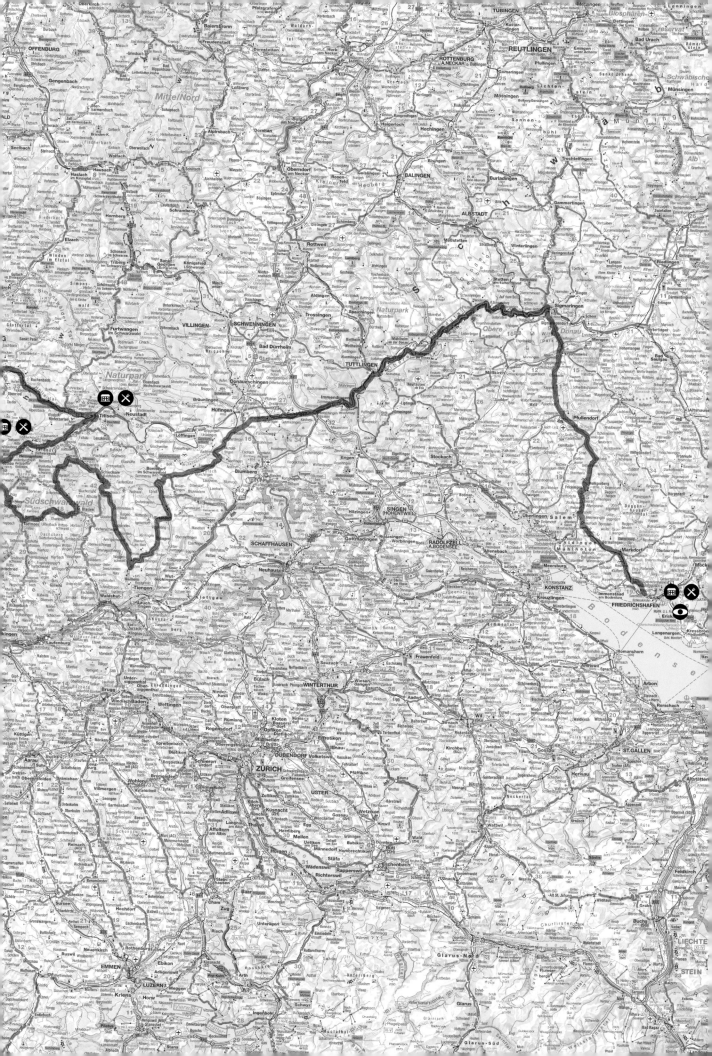

FRIEDRICHS-HAFEN
TEGERNSEE

443 KM • 9 STUNDEN // 275 MILES • 9 HOURS

Schimmernde Aluminiumhaut, mächtige Tragflächen, feiste Nieten, hölzerne Propeller – es dauert beim Rundgang durch das Dornier Museum in Friedrichshafen eine Weile, bis du verstehst, welche Geschichte die Luftfahrt-Ikone Dornier mit dem Bodensee verbindet. Claude Dornier, Versuchsingenieur bei Zeppelin mit Entwicklungsauftrag zum Bau von Tragflächen-Flugzeugen, ließ sich von der enormen Fläche des Bodensees inspirieren.

—

Shiny aluminum panels, mighty wings, stout rivets, wooden propellers – it takes a while to tour the Dornier Museum in Friedrichshafen before you understand the history that connects the aviation icon Dornier with Lake Constance. Claude Dornier, a Zeppelin engineer with a development contract to construct a hydrofoil aircraft, was inspired by the enormous expanse of Lake Constance.

HOTEL

ALPENLOGE
KIRCHENANGER 6
88175 SCHEIDEGG
ALLGÄU / BAYERN
WWW.ALPENLOGE.COM
WWW.PRETTY-HOTELS.COM

Wo auch immer es Seen, breite Flüsse und Kanäle oder Meeresbuchten gibt, könnte ein Wasserflugzeug landen – überall auf der Welt. Dornier konstruierte und baute also Flugboote, regelrechte Giganten mit vielen Motoren, hochgesetzten oder Doppeldecker-Tragflächen und gepfeilten Rümpfen. 1917 wurde die Flugzeug-Abteilung des alten Grafen Zeppelin unter der Leitung Claude Dorniers eigenständig, und eine turbulente Erfolgsgeschichte dieser Pionierzeiten begann mit Giganten wie dem „Wal" oder der „Do X". Erst der Zweite Weltkrieg bremste Dornier aus, die Firma musste Flugmaschinen für die deutsche Luftwaffe konstruieren – am Ende des Kriegs war Dornier am Boden. Die finanziell ausgeblutete Firma musste sich nun einem internationalen Wettbewerb stellen, für den sie nicht mehr auf ihren in den 1920er-und 1930er-Jahren erarbeiteten Vorsprung zurückgreifen konnte. Die Luftfahrt hatte sich aus ihren wagemutigen Teenager-Jahren in ein Boom-Zeitalter hinein entwickelt, Dornier stand ein rauer Ritt bevor, denn in den Achtzigerjahren wurde das Unternehmen schließlich von Daimler-Benz übernommen.

Der Südwesten Deutschlands scheint jedenfalls ein ideales Klima für Erfinder und Innovatoren zu haben. Es sind allerdings nicht die großen Weltkonzerne Baden-Württembergs, Mercedes-Benz, Porsche oder Bosch, die das eigentliche Rad drehen, sondern die vielen Mittelständler: inhabergeführte Hightechunternehmen der Maschinen- und Elektronikbranche, die mit nur wenigen hundert Angestellten in der ganzen Welt aktiv sind. Nach wie vor machen sie die Pace, stehen für „Made in Germany" und prägen den Ruf eines ganzen Landes. Man könnte viel darüber spekulieren, worin diese Umtriebigkeit und Erfinderfreude fußen – wir sind überzeugt: Es liegt an der Lage. Viele Jahrhunderte gab es hier außer Land- und Forstwirtschaft kaum etwas zu holen, die ganze Zeit aber wurde der Süden Deutschlands von ständigem Kommen und Gehen befruchtet. In diesem Klima wächst das Um-die-Ecke-denken, man hat gehört, man hat gesehen, man beginnt, an Möglichkeiten zu glauben und vermeintliche Unmöglichkeiten in Frage zu stellen. Wenn es eine Kernkompetenz der Süddeutschen gibt,

Wherever there are lakes, wide rivers, canals or bays, seaplanes could land – anywhere in the world. Dornier designed and built flying boats, veritable giants with multiple engines, high-mounted or double-deck wings and tapered fuselages. In 1917, the aircraft department of the old Count Ferdinand von Zeppelin became independent under the direction of Claude Dornier, ushering in a tumultuous success story of those pioneering times with giants like the "Wal" and the "Do X". However, the Second World War put a damper on Dornier, with the company conscripted to design aircraft for the German Luftwaffe – and by the end of the war, the company was on its knees. The financially-drained enterprise now had to face international competition; they could no longer fall back on their advantage gained in the 1920s and 1930s. From its daring early years, aviation had become a boom industry. Dornier was in for a rough ride. In the 1980s the company was finally taken over by Daimler-Benz.

In any case, the southwest of Germany seems to have an ideal climate for inventors and innovators. However, it is not the large global corporations of Bad-Württemberg, like Mercedes-Benz, Porsche or Bosch, that turn the wheels, but the many medium-sized companies: owner-managed high-tech enterprises in the machinery and electronics industries that employ just a few hundred people for their global operations. They still set the pace; they represent Made in Germany and shape the reputation of an entire country. One could speculate about the reason behind this activity and inventiveness – we, however, are convinced that it is the location. For centuries, this region had very little to offer apart from agriculture and forestry, but with the constant comings and goings in Germany's south, new ideas flourished. In this climate, lateral thinking blooms, someone heard, someone saw – and eventually one begins to believe in possibilities and to question whether the impossible is, in fact, possible. If there is a core competence of the southern German, then it is this: "keep moving" – in mind or body, voluntarily or out of necessity. The world doesn't stop at the Alps – it goes all the way to Sicily. The world down here reaches to the Volga, after all, boats can

st es das Unterwegssein. Im Kopf oder auf en Beinen, freiwillig oder auf der Flucht. is Sizilien reicht die Welt hier unten, sie ndet nicht an den Alpen. Bis an die Wol- a reicht die Welt hier unten, denn Boote önnen mit der Donau ins Schwarze Meer ahren und dort über den Don nach Osten. is über den Atlantik reicht Deutschlands üden, denn er hat seine hungernden Kin- er auf der Suche nach Perspektiven in die erne getrieben. Und das alles sind keine Geschichten voller Pathos, sondern voller Mühsal. Es sind keine klar in Gut und Böse ingeteilte Geschichten, sondern man weiß ier, dass Helden und Schurken oft ein- und lasselbe sind. Man kennt die Geschichten ler Schwabenkinder, die im Sommer von hren Eltern aus den Alpentälern nach Nor- len geschickt wurden, um – beinahe wie klaven – den schwäbischen Bauern als rntehelfer zu dienen. Wenn überhaupt für inen Hungerlohn, oft aber nur für karge Kost und Prügel. Diese Szenen kennen wir eute noch aus den Schwellenländern die- er Erde. Sie scheinen uns weit weg, aber sie ind nur einen Atemzug weit entfernt von len blühenden, lieblichen Landschaften chwabens und des Allgäus. Heute, wenn vir über die ersten Pässe am Alpenrand ahren, werden wir an sie denken, die klei- nen, heimwehkranken Berg-Kinder, nach Norden wandernd im Schlepptau größerer Geschwister. Ihr Schicksal gehört zu die- em Land wie die Schönheit und die Liebe. Vielleicht ist es ja sogar so, dass die peni- bel gepflegten Vorgärten, die geranienge- chmückten Balkone, die sauberen Ort- chaften im kollektiven Wissen um das iemals weit entfernte Chaos entstehen.

Hinter Lindau endet der Bodensee, seine enorme Wasserfläche hat uns die ganze Zeit in einiger Entfernung begleitet, und etzt tritt das flache Land zurück. Die Berge les Bregenzerwaldes türmen sich auf, und noch stürmen wir sie in wenigen Schwün- gen. Die Bundesstraße 308 nennt sich mit offiziellem Diplom des Tourismusverbands „Alpenstraße" und stellt mit ein paar ers- en, derbe eingestreuten Serpentinen hi- nüber nach Lindenberg im Allgäu klar, was lamit gemeint ist: aussichtsreiches Fahren nklusive schmackhafter Kurvenunterhal- ung. Aber die Alpenstraße kann gelegent- ich auch etwas zu domestiziert daher-

travel down the Danube into the Black Sea and from there over the Don River to the east. Germany's south stretches over the Atlantic because it had driven its starving children far away in search of perspective. These stories are not full of pathos, rath- er they tell of hardship. These tales are not clearly divided into good and evil, but one realizes here that heroes and villains are often one and the same. We know the sto- ries of the Swabian children who were sent north from the Alpine valleys by their par- ents in summer to help with the harvest, virtually as slaves to the Swabian farm- ers – earning a pittance if they were lucky, but more often than not, working for scraps of food and a beating. We recognize these scenes today from the emerging countries of the world, they seem far away to us, but they are only a breath away from the blos- soming, picturesque landscapes of Swabia and the Allgäu. Today, when we drive over the first passes at the edge of the Alps, we will think of them, the small, homesick mountain children, walking north in the shadow of their older siblings. Their fate is as tied to this country as beauty and love. Perhaps it could even be said that the me- ticulously maintained gardens, the gerani- um-decorated balconies, the tidy villages, have evolved from the collective knowledge of the chaos that is never far away.

Lake Constance ends after Lindau, its enor- mous expanse of water has been our faithful companion for some distance, and now the flat land is left behind. The mountains of the Bregenz Forest swell up and we take them by storm in a few swings. The federal high- way 308 has been given the tourism associ- ation's official stamp as the "Alpenstraße", and, with a couple of liberally strewn ser- pentines across to Lindenberg im Allgäu, the reason becomes evident: view-stud- ded driving including delicious cornering entertainment. But the Alpenstraße can sometimes be a little too tame when being merciful on passengers' weak stomachs or when luring its travelers all too obviously to the tourist attractions and to the city cen- ters for a spot of shopping. Sometimes it pays to mistrust the routing, so we defiant- ly turn south at Scheidegg and continue on small roads with its clusters of villages towards the east. A region with a relaxed

HOTELS

DAS KRANZBACH
HOTEL & WELLNESS-REFUGIUM
KRANZBACH/KLAIS
WWW.DASKRANZBACH.DE
WWW.PRETTY-HOTELS.COM

SCHLOSS ELMAU
IN ELMAU 2
82493 KRÜN
WWW.SCHLOSS-ELMAU.DE

QUARTIER
ST.-MARTIN-STRASSE 26
82467 GARMISCH-PARTENKIRCHEN
WWW.QUARTIER-GAPA.DE

kommen, wenn sie Rücksicht auf schwache Mägen der Beifahrer nehmen oder ihre Reisenden allzu offensichtlich zu den touristischen Attraktionen und in die zum Shopping einladenden Innenstädte lotsen möchte. Etwas Misstrauen gegenüber der Routenführung ist von Zeit zu Zeit also durchaus angesagt, deshalb biegen wir bei Scheidegg ganz trotzig nach Süden ab und fahren dann über kleine Straßen und wenige Häuser große Weiler in östlicher Richtung weiter. Ein Land mit entspanntem Ruhepuls tut sich auf, voller bunter Details und kleiner Geschichten, wir sind ganz nah bei den Leuten.

In Hinterstaufen sind wir zurück auf der 308, schnüren in entspanntem Trab weiter und passieren nach wenigen Kilometern den Großen Alpsee, überqueren bei Immenstadt die Iller und folgen dem Fluss in einiger Entfernung nach Süden bis Sonthofen. Hier im südlichen Allgäu drängen sich die Alpen mit Macht gegen ihr Vorland. Aus der Vogelperspektive könnte man jetzt einen ausgezeichneten Blick auf Erdgeschichte in Millionen-Jahre-Zeitlupe werfen: Vor einem Augenzwinkern erst waren die Alpen von mächtigen Gletschern bedeckt, lediglich die hohen Gipfel des Gebirges überragten den Eispanzer, und der zog sich weit nach Norden. Schrammte über den Boden darunter, hobelte und warf Wellen. Man darf sich Gletscher nicht als träge daliegende Phlegmatiker vorstellen, sie sind ungestüm wie junge Hunde und stark wie Wasserstoffbomben. Wenn das Eis knackend und knirschend durch das Land darunter marodiert, bleibt kein Stein auf dem anderen. Irgendwann aber müssen sie gehen. In Erdzeitaltern gemessen gehören die Gletscher der europäischen Eiszeit zu eher kurzlebigen Erscheinungen, allerdings haben sie es in ein paar Jahrtausenden hin oder her tatsächlich geschafft, eine Welt zu formen. Die letzten Auswirkungen

pulse opens up, full of colorful details and anecdotes, and we're very close to the people. We rejoin the 308 at Hinterstaufen and continue on at an easy pace, pass the Großer Alpsee, cross the Iller at Immenstadt and follow the river for some time to the south until Sonthofen. Here in the south of the Allgäu, the Alps press hard against the foreland. From a bird's eye perspective, you could now get a good look at the history of the Earth in slow motion over millions of years: not so long ago, the Alps were blanketed in mighty glaciers, with only the tips of the mountain tops peeking out from an icy mantle that stretched far to the north. Gouging the ground below, grating as it advanced and throwing up waves on the way. Glaciers are not to be regarded as sloth-like and phlegmatic; they are impetuous like puppies and powerful like hydrogen bombs. When the ice groans and graunches, marauding through the land as it goes, no stone is left unturned. But at some point, they have to vanish. Measured in geological terms, the glaciers of the European ice age belong to rather short-lived phenomena, but within a few odd millennia, they have indeed managed to shape a world. We still see the lingering evidence of the great grinding and crushing: Almost all lakes in the Alpine foothills are the melted remains of the ice age and the undulating, hilly countryside of the Allgäu is the old glacial bed.

Whoever goes by land never travels over a plain, but is constantly traversing the strangely rolling countryside, on which lush grasses grow, lucky cows graze and hardy folks live. The people of the Allgäu are a story in themselves. Defiantly they frolic between Swabia and Bavaria, blessed with great fortitude and business acumen, enormous love of heimat and dry humor. You gotta love'em. With Bad Hindelang behind us, now we can shift down

les großen Schleifens und Mahlens bekommen wir noch mit: Nahezu alle Seen des Alpenvorlands sind geschmolzene Reste der Eiszeit, und das wellige, hügelige Land des Allgäus ist das alte Bett des Gletschers. Wer im Boden unterwegs ist, bewegt sich niemals durch eine flache Ebene, sondern ist immer von eigentümlich welligem Gelände umgeben, auf dem üppiges Gas wächst, glückliche Kühe grasen und ein knorriger Menschenschlag lebt. Die Allgäuer sind ein Kapitel für sich, trotzig tummeln sie sich zwischen Schwaben und Bayern, mit großer Energie und Geschäftstüchtigkeit, enormer Heimatliebe und trockenem Humor gesegnet. Man muss sie mögen. Bad Hindelang ist vorüber, jetzt darf ein Gang zurückgeschaltet werden: Auf zum Oberjochpass. Mit lässigem Takt fegt der in grünen Wiesen den Berg hinauf und wieder hinunter, wer sich danach verfährt, landet in dieser Gegend immer in Österreich. Schließlich ist die Grenze zum Nachbarstaat seit dem Bodensee immer beinahe in Rufweite. Wir fahren nach Norden bis Wertach, halten uns südlich des Grüntensees und schlagen in Nesselwang erneut wieder einen Weg in südöstlicher Richtung ein. Zwischen Weißensee und Hopfensee hindurch landen wir in Füssen. Und jetzt stellt sich uns die Gretchenfrage: Neuschwanstein, ja oder nein?

Man muss in Bayern – und hierher haben wir es mittlerweile geschafft – sehr aufpassen, wenn man über König Ludwig II. spricht. Auch wenn die Bayern mittlerweile lupenreine Demokraten und ganz und gar in der großen Bundesrepublik Deutschland angekommen sind, haben sie eben doch immer wieder eine unerklärliche Schwäche für die guten, alten Zeiten der Monarchie, als man noch mit „den Preußen" auf Kriegsfuß lag. „Die Preußen", das sind in Bayern nicht etwa nur die Deutschen rund um das 600 Kilometer weiter nördlich gelegene Berlin, sondern vermutlich geht man hier selbst als Ainu, Aborigine oder Sioux als „Preuße" durch. Der Vollständigkeit halber wird man dann liebevoll als „Saupreuß" klassifiziert, darf das gerne als freundschaftliches Schmäh-Kompliment nehmen – aber eben dennoch niemals schlecht über Ludwig II. reden. Dass der geistig stets etwas fragile König der Bayern eine ähnliche Entwicklung wie Elvis Presley durchgemacht hatte und gegen Ende

a gear and up to the Oberjoch Pass. At an easy gait, the pass road sweeps up the green meadows of the mountain and down again. All wrong turns in the region end up in Austria: the border to the neighboring state has always been within shouting distance of Lake Constance. We head north to Wertach, keeping south of Lake Grünten and strike out from Nesselwang again in a south-easterly direction. Between the Weißensee and Hopfensee lakes, we end up in Fuessen and now the crucial question: Neuschwanstein, Ja or Nein?

You have to be careful in Bavaria – where we've now arrived – when talking about King Ludwig II. Even though the Bavarians are now pure democrats and have completely embraced the great Federal Republic of Germany, they still have an inexplicable soft-spot for the good old days of the monarchy, when they were on bad terms with the "Prussians". In Bavaria, "the Prussians" are not only the Germans around Berlin 600 kilometers or so further north, but apparently, even if you're an Ainu, Aborigine or Sioux, you are considered a Prussian here. For the sake of completeness, it would be rough but well-meaning to be called a "Saupreuß" (literal translation: sow-Prussian) – but, whatever you do, never speak ill of Ludwig II. The fact that the mentally somewhat fragile King of the Bavarians suffered a similar fate to Elvis Presley and turned up towards the end of his career wearing glittery suits as a parody of a king, is unimportant to the Bavarians. For them, Ludwig II will always be the slim, mentally sound Bavarian hero par excellence. It's Now or Never.

Neuschwanstein is the Graceland of the late Ludwig II, so to speak. Here, he lived out his most plush fantasies. The castle has no real historical background, but even during its construction at Ludwig's behest, it was intended as a kind of backdrop for a lofty royal lifestyle. All this would warrant an amusing visit, but unfortunately, thousands of tourists from all over the world think the same year after year. Either visit in winter or be prepared to queue. Like us, of course. And, of course, we buy the mug with the portrait of the unfortunate Ludwig and the miniature Neuschwanstein in a snow globe. "Mia san mia," says the Pakistan-born

HOTEL & RESTAURANT

BACHMAIR WEISSACH SPA & RESORT
WIESSEER STR. 1
83700 ROTTACH-EGERN
WWW.BACHMAIR-WEISSACH.COM

HOTEL BUSSI BABY
SANKTJOHANSERSTRASSE 46
83707 BAD WIESSEE
WWW.BUSSIBABY.COM

einer Karriere gerne im Glitzeranzug als Parodie eines Königs auftrat, ist den Bayern unwichtig, für sie wird Ludwig II. stets der schlanke, geistig kerngesunde Bayern-Held schlechthin bleiben. It's now or never. Neuschwanstein, das ist sozusagen das Graceland des späten Ludwig II., hier lebte er seine plüschigsten Fantasien aus. Das Schloss hat keinen wirklich historischen Hintergrund, sondern war bereits bei seiner Entstehung auf Geheiß Ludwigs als eine Art Kulisse für das königlich-ästhetische Lebensgefühl gedacht. All das wäre ja noch immer einen amüsierten Besuch wert, dummerweise beschließen diesen Jahr für Jahr viele tausend Touristen aus aller Welt. Man kommt also entweder im Winter oder bringt eine gewisse Lust am Schlangestehen mit. – Natürlich tun wir es. Natürlich kaufen wir auch die Tasse mit dem Konterfei des unglücklichen Ludwig und das Miniaturschloss-Neuschwanstein in der Schneekugel. „Mia san mia", sagt der aus Pakistan stammende Verkäufer, als er uns alles in eine weiß-blau-gemusterte Tüte packt, und seine Zähne blitzen wunderbar weiß dabei.

Die Fluchtroute nach Norden entlang des Forggensees, über Steingaden bis Murnau am Staffelsee steht Neuschwanstein in Sachen Dramatik glücklicherweise in nichts nach, zwischen Steingaden und Wildsteig sind wir touristisch sogar wieder soweit regeneriert und außerhalb der direkten Kitsch-Todeszone, dass wir selbst den Abstecher zur Wieskirche schaffen. Der lohnt sich wirklich, und ab dann sind das Land und die Straße völlig reale und bodenständige Hauptattraktionen. Über die Kesselbergstraße zwischen Kochel- und Walchensee geht es mit Schwung und Verve, dann turnen wir bis weit nach Süden zum Schloss Elmau. Die wilde, kalte Isar in ihrem steinigen Bett reißt uns mit bis Vorderriß, und dann stürmen wir hier sogar noch zur Stippvisite am großen Ahornboden über die Grenze nach Österreich. Wer ins Tal möchte, kann nur von Norden kommend hinein – in ein abgeschiedenes Tal wie der Tagtraum eines anderen Planeten. Abendlicht schwebt, die umgebenden Berge werfen lange Schatten auf den Talgrund und beugen die Sonnenstrahlen in eine gläserne Aura. Zurück zum türkisblauen Sylvensteinsee, der im Gebirge liegt wie ein erschütternd majestätisch inszeniertes Motiv aus Werbefilmen, dann segeln wir über Jachenau und schmale Sträßchen ans Ostufer des Walchensees für eine erneute Kehrtwende –, wir können einfach nicht genug von dieser Fahrt bekommen. Es geht wieder für ein paar Kilometer dicht an der Grenze zu Österreich entlang, dann schwenkt die Straße in Wildbad Kreuth nach Norden ab. Wir folgen ihr beinahe schlafwandlerisch, während ein mit Schönheit gefüllter Tag in den Abend hineinsickert. Und jetzt sehen wir das Ende der Etappe direkt vor uns: Rottach-Egern am Tegernsee. Bayern wie es nicht echter sein könnte. Urwüchsig und stark, freundlich und filterlos und – ganz ohne König.

„Mia san mia", sagt der aus Pakistan stammende Verkäufer, als er uns alles in eine weiß-blau-gemusterte Tüte packt, und seine Zähne blitzen wunderbar weiß dabei.

"Mia san mia," says the Pakistan-born salesman with a flash of his pearly white teeth as he wraps everything in a white-and-blue checkered bag.

salesman with a flash of his pearly white teeth as he wraps everything in a white-and-blue checkered bag. The escape route to the north along Lake Forggensee via Steingaden to Murnau am Staffelsee is thankfully in no way inferior to Neuschwanstein in terms of drama; between Steingaden and Wildsteig we're even touristically rejuvenated enough and have stepped so far beyond the death-by-kitsch zone that we decide to take the detour to the Pilgrimage Church of Wies. It's truly worthwhile, and from this point on the country and the road become the very real and down-to-earth main attractions. We follow the Kesselbergstraße between Kochelsee and Walchensee with power and verve, then take a long vault far south to Elmau Castle. The wild, cold Isar in its stony bed sweeps us as far as Vorderriss, from here we storm to Grosser Ahornboden to make a flying visit over the border to Austria. The valley can only be reached from the north – a remote valley like a daydream of another planet. Evening light floods in, the surrounding mountains cast long shadows on the valley floor and bend the sun's rays into a luminous aura.

Back to the glacial turquoise Sylvensteinsee, cupped in the mountains like a majestically staged advertising motif, we then sail over the Jachenau and along the narrow roads to the eastern shore of the Walchensee before making a U-turn – we simply can't get enough of this drive. We continue for another few kilometers hugging the border to Austria before the road turns north at Wildbad Kreuth. We follow it almost like sleepwalkers, as a day filled with beauty seeps into the evening. Now we can see the end of the leg right in front of us: Rottach-Egern at Lake Tegernsee. Bavaria as real as it could ever be. Unspoilt and strong, friendly and unfiltered – and totally kingless.

AWARD WINNING PAPER

BÜTTENPAPIERFABRIK
GMUND GMBH & CO. KG
MANGFALLSTRASSE 5
83703 GMUND AM TEGERNSEE
TEL +49 (80 22) 75 00-0
WWW.GMUND.COM

....

FRIEDRICHSHAFEN TEGERNSEE

Mit seiner enormen Wasserfläche gilt der Bodensee in Deutschland als das Meer der Schwaben – ein etwas vereinnahmender Titel, wenn man weiß, das sein südliches Ufer in der Schweiz liegt und das östliche Ende bei Bregenz zu Österreich gehört. Und bei unserem Etappenstart in Friedrichshafen lässt sich sowieso kaum verbergen, dass die Bodensee-Region alles andere als provinziell ist: Industrie und Technologie gehören schon seit Menschengedenken in diese Ecke. Es dauert viele Kilometer, bis wir den riesigen See hinter uns gelassen haben und dann über den Bregenzerwald ins liebliche Allgäu vorgestoßen sind. Wir streifen diese bemerkenswerte Gegend weit im Süden, hier geht eine uralte Kulturlandschaft mit ganz eigenem Charakter bereits in alpines Gelände über. Hinter Pfronten sind wir dann in Bayern gelandet und rollen entlang der sich immer höher aufbäumenden Berge weiter nach Osten. Mit dem Schloss Neuschwanstein legen wir einen höchst touristischen Zwischenstopp ein – oder lassen ihn aus und konzentrieren uns auf das reine Fahren. Die schmelzenden Gletscher der letzten Eiszeit haben hier die berühmten Seen Oberbayerns hinterlassen: Mit Forggensee und Walchensee erleben wir nicht nur die größten –, entlang der Isar und Weißach geht es dann immer weiter in den Osten, bis wir am Tegernsee das Ende unserer Etappe erreichen.

—

With its huge expanse of water, Lake Constance in Germany is known as the Swabian Sea – a somewhat possessive title considering its southern shore is in Switzerland and the eastern end at Bregenz belongs to Austria. Yet, at the start of this leg in Friedrichshafen, it is very clear that the Lake Constance region is anything but provincial: industry and technology have been part of this corner for as long as people can remember. It takes many kilometers until we've left the huge lake behind us, and continue on to the Bregenz Forest into the delightful Allgäu. We sweep over this remarkable area far to the south, where an ancient cultural landscape with its own character merges into Alpine terrain. After Pfronten we end up in Bavaria and roll further east along the mountains, which tower higher and higher. Neuschwanstein Castle offers a very touristy stopover – or skip it and enjoy the pure driving experience. The melting glaciers of the last ice age have left the famous lakes of Upper Bavaria here, with Forggensee and Walchensee we experience some of the smaller ones – along the Isar and the Weißach we continue east until we reach the end of this leg at Lake Tegernsee.

443 KM • 9 STUNDEN // 275 MILES • 9 HOURS

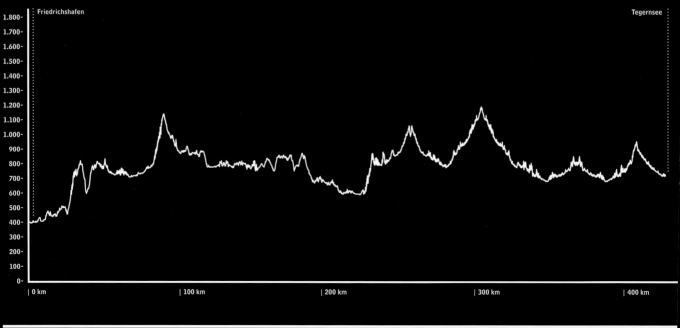

TEGERNSEE BERCHTES-GADEN

210 KM • 5 STUNDEN // 131 MILES • 5 HOURS

Aufwachen in Bayern. Da fragst du dich immer wieder mal, ob die Leute hier eigentlich noch sehen, wie gut sie es haben. Nicht nur das Land ist voller Kraft, auch die Bayern an sich gehören zu einem äußerst angenehmen Menschenschlag. Sie sind ideenreich und detailverliebt, darüber hinaus haben sie einen Blick für die schönen Seiten des Lebens.

—

Waking up in Bavaria, you keep asking yourself whether the people here truly realize just how blessed they are. Not only is the land powerful, but the Bavarians themselves are also extremely pleasant people, full of ideas and a love of detail, with an eye for the beautiful things of life.

HOTEL & RESTAURANT

TANNERHOF
TANNERHOFSTRASSE 32
83735 BAYRISCHZELL
WWW.NATUR-HOTEL-TANNERHOF.DE

Bayern, das ist ein Herzensland. – Wir stehen in der Büttenpapierfabrik in Gmund am Tegernsee und freuen uns von Mundwinkel zu Mundwinkel, strahlen wie Kinder. Genießen das Rascheln und den seidigen Griff des Papiers, die pastelligen Farben, den mürben Glanz, die zarte und gleichzeitig eigenwillige Materialität. Dass man aus Holz tolle Dinge machen kann, wussten wir. Dass Papier aus Holz gemacht wird, wussten wir ebenfalls. Aber dann muss man anscheinend an einem solchen Ort vorbeikommen, um etwas ansonsten Selbstverständliches ganz neu zu entdecken: Papier, einfach nur Papier. In diesem Moment völlig außergewöhnlich, beinahe ein Wunder.

Wenn Tage auf der Straße auf diese Weise starten, dauert es lange, bis der Adrenalinstoß des Schönen und Guten nachlässt. Bis irgendetwas wieder einfach nur ganz gewöhnlich ist. Plötzlich spürst du alles ganz neu und stark, die Farben werden bunter, die Düfte intensiver. Dunkelgrün marschieren mächtige Berge rund um den Tegernsee heran und scharen sich um seine weite Fläche wie struppige, neugierige Riesen, während sich das Wasser des Sees in Schattierungen von Braun bis Türkis der Umzingelung entgegenstemmt. Mürber Duft nach süßem Wasser steigt auf, das frisch gemähte Gras der Wiesen ringsum verströmt Würzigkeit, aus den Waldhängen sickert das Aroma von Harz und Holz. Weiß und schwarz sind die Häuser der Ortschaften, in allen Farben bunt und energiegeladen die Lüftel-Malereien an den Hauswänden. Das gibt es in Schwaben und Baden nicht, hier wird erneut die Nähe Bayerns zu Italien sichtbar. Geschichten aus dem Alltagsleben spielen sich an den Fassaden der Häuser ab, Szenen aus biblischen Erzählungen, illustrierte Segenssprüche und bauernschlaue Moritaten finden ebenso einen Platz. Hell- und grasgrün breiten sich Felder und Weiden aus, die von Baumreihen und Bächen eingerahmt sind, und mittendrin strebt eine Straße im munteren Rhythmus eines Zither-und-Akkordeon-Schuhplattlers mit solide wetterndem Tuba-Bass nach Osten. Rüber nach Hausham und am Schliersee vorbei, die dort ansässige Whisky-Destillerie lassen wir schweren Herzens links liegen. Don't drink and drive. Das heißt –

Bavaria is a heartland. We visit the handmade paper factory in Gmund am Tegernsee, beaming like kids in a candy store. We savor the rustle and silky feel of the paper, the pastel colors, the matte luster, the delicate yet willful texture. We knew that beautiful things could be crafted out of wood, we also knew that paper was made of wood, but then you visit such a place and rediscover something that you normally take for granted: paper, just paper, suddenly becomes completely extraordinary, almost miraculous.

When days on the road start like this, it takes a long time for the adrenaline rush from all things good and beautiful to subside. Until it all becomes just plain ordinary again. Suddenly you see everything in a new and bright light, colors are more colorful, scents more intense. Mighty, dark green mountains rise out of Lake Tegernsee and hug its vastness like shaggy, curious giants, while the lake braces itself against the encroachment in hues of brown to turquoise. A heady scent of forest and sweet water rises from the lake, the herbaceous fragrance of freshly mown grass envelops us, the aroma of resin and wood wafts from the forested slopes. The village houses are black and white, the fresco paintings on the outside walls all colors of the rainbow. No such thing exists in Swabia and Baden, here again, the closeness to Italy is noticeable. Stories from everyday life are played out on the facades of the houses, scenes from biblical stories, illustrated blessings and everyday morality also find expression. Light green and lush, the fields and pastures spread out, framed by streams and rows of trees, and the road marches to the east in the lively rhythm of a zither and accordion Schuhplattler with a solid weatherproof tuba bass. Over to Hausham and past Lake Schliersee, where, with heavy hearts, we drive straight past a whiskey distillery. Don't drink and drive. But hang on a minute: we could always put a bottle in the trunk for a very special occasion… handbrake slide and return. The deep, woody scent of the Slyrs alone is worth the stop. We're back on the Alpenstraße and for now, we have no objections to its course. Especially since it pushes into the moun-

inen Moment mal: Man könnte sich eine Flasche ja uch ins Gepäck stecken, für ganze besondere Stunden ..., Iandbremswende und zurück. Allein der mächtige, ölzerne, tiefe Duft des „Slyrs" ist einen Stopp wert. Wir ind wieder auf der Alpenstraße unterwegs, und fürs Erste aben wir überhaupt keine Einwände zu ihrem Verlauf. chon gar nicht, seit sie sich hinter Bayrischzell in die Ber- e verdrückt hat, auf den Sudelfeldpass mit seinen Ser- entinen und Bögen und den Cinemascope-Ausblicken. n den Tatzelwurm-Wasserfällen ist uns die Alpenstraße nit ihrem eifrigen Fokus aufs Ziel am östlichen Ende Bay- rns und Deutschlands aber wieder einmal zu zielstrebig. nstatt ihr nach Osten in Richtung Oberaudorf zu folgen, iehen wir genüsslich nach Norden und fahren weiter auf er mautpflichtigen Tatzelwurmstraße. Dass sich dieses tück konzentriert kurvigen Asphalts nach einem mys- ischen Drachen-Untier nennt, liegt ganz augenscheinlich her am Namen der benachbarten Wasserfälle, als am haraktor der Streckenführung: Ruhig und ohne große ahrerische Schwierigkeitsgrade fließt der Tatzelwurm ahin, lehnt sich an Berghänge, schneidet zwar manch- nal seinen Lauf fordernd ins Terrain, bleibt aber immer uf der milden und deeskalierenden Seite. Eher Mate- ial für einen Howard-Shore-Soundtrack, als für das LCD oundsystem-Mixtape. Magische Momente und wohltem- erierter Groove bringen den freundlichen Drachen auf den ücken eines bewaldeten Bergmassivs und wohlbehalten n seiner Rückseite wieder hinunter – ins Inn-Tal.

3ei Brannenburg stranden wir am Ufer, der je nach Jah- eszeit eisgrün, kalkweiß oder lehmbraun dahinziehen- e Inn hat an dieser Stelle bereits den größten Teil seiner nsgesamt rund 500 Kilometer langen Reise geschafft, er ührt nun das Wasser aus einem riesigen Alpenraum mit ich. Hat die eiskalte Energie von Gletschern, Schneegip- eln und unzähligen Gebirgsbächen in sich aufgenom- nen und das spürt man ihm ab: Drängend schiebt er vo- an, rastlos und unerbittlich. Zähneknirschend vor Staub, lackernd mit Geröll und Schutt. Seit seinem Ursprung in en Schweizer Alpen bei Sankt Moritz liegen bereits zwei ändergrenzen hinter ihm, in ein oder zwei Tagen wird as Wasser des Inn bei Passau in der Donau landen und o eines der größten Flußsysteme Europas speisen – Rei- e, Reise, wohin wir auch schauen. Nach einem kurzen prung über den Samerberg und dessen ruhiger Land- chaft, landen wir an einem großen Lauf der ganz ande- en Art: Die Autobahn A 8 rollt aus dem Westen kommend eran, 370 Kilometer hat sie seit ihrem Beginn bei Karls- uhe im Rheintal zurückgelegt und ist dabei auf ihrem Kurs oberhalb des Schwarzwalds, nördlich der Schwäbi- chen Alb und des Allgäus genau an derselben Stelle ge- andet wie wir. Neugierig schauen wir auf den endlosen Strom der Autos und stellen uns vor, wie es wäre, jetzt infach die letzten 60 Kilometer zur Grenze nach Öster- eich auf ihr abzukürzen. In etwas über einer halben

tains after Bayrischzell, to the Sudelfeld Pass with its serpentines and hairpins and cinemascope views. At the Tatzelwurm Waterfalls, the Alpenstraße, with its eager focus on the destination at the eastern end of Bavaria and Germany, once again proves too resolute for us. In- stead of heading east towards Oberaudorf, we happily drive north, following the Tatzelwurm toll road. The fact that this piece of tightly-twisting asphalt is named after a mystical dragon is apparently due to the neighboring waterfalls rather than the nature of the road: the Tatzel- wurm stretch flows languidly and without any great effort, leaning against the mountainside, at times carving its course into the terrain but always staying on the mild, de-escalation side. More suited to a Howard Shore soundtrack than an LCD Soundsystem mixtape. Magi- cal moments and a well-tempered groove lift the friendly dragon to the ridge of the forested mountain range and safely over the other side and down into the Inn Valley. At Brannenburg we strand on the shore: icy green, chal- ky white or muddy brown – depending on the season – the Inn river has already covered most of its 500-kilometer journey at this point, and now carries the water from a huge Alpine region. It has absorbed the ice-cold energy of glaciers, snow peaks and countless mountain streams, and this is palpable: gushing forward, restless and re- lentless. Gnashing on dust, clattering with rock and rub- ble. Since its origin in the Swiss Alps near St. Moritz, it has flowed across two national borders, in a day or so the waters of the Inn will arrive near Passau in the Danube to feed one of the largest river systems in Europe – on- ward, onward, wherever we look.

After a short hop over the Samerberg and its peaceful landscape, we end up observing a long-run of a com- pletely different kind: The A 8 autobahn approaches from the west, it has covered 370 kilometers since its start near Karlsruhe in the Rhine Valley, and it is heading to the top of the Black Forest, north of the Swabian Jura and the Allgäu to end up at the exact same spot where we now stand. We curiously watch the endless stream of cars and imagine what it would be like to shorten the last 60 kilometers to the Austrian border. In a little over half an hour, we would be at the end of our journey from west to east. But there is still so much to discov- er: the Alps of the Karwendel Mountains magically call us. First, however, we veer south of the Chiemsee to the east, the road is guided by the shores of the prime- val lake: on the left, alluvial floodplains stretch to the Chiemsee, on the right the topography buckles towards the mountains. It's a pity that there are no time ma- chines in which we can drift to the end of the ice age and watch the great melting of the ice sheets in fast motion. Today's Chiemsee with its 80 square kilometers would be the last puddle – and if we accidentally left our finger on the fast forward button for 3,000, 4,000, 5,000 years, we

HOTEL & RESTAURANT

CHIEMGAUHOF
JULIUS-EXTER-PROMENADE 21
3236 ÜBERSEE
WWW.CHIEMGAUHOF.COM

Stunde wären wir am Ende der Reise von West nach Ost. Aber da gibt es noch so viel zu entdecken, die Alpen des Karwendelgebirges locken uns magisch an. Aber zuerst steuern wir südlich des Chiemsees nach Osten, die Straße lässt sich vom Verlauf des urzeitlichen Seeufers dirigieren: Links breiten sich Schwemmland-Auen bis zum Chiemsee aus, rechts buckelt die Topografie in Richtung der Berge. Schade, dass es keine Zeitmaschinen gibt, in denen man sich bis ans Ende der Eiszeit treiben lassen kann, um dann im Zeitraffer das große Schmelzen des Eispanzers zu verfolgen. Der heutige Chiemsee mit seinen 80 Quadratkilometern wäre lediglich eine letzte Pfütze – und wenn wir den Finger aus Versehen 3000, 4000 oder 5000 Jahre zu lange auf der Zeitmaschinen-Vorspultaste ließen, könnten wir erstaunt verfolgen, wie die Pfütze weiter verdunstet.

Bei Marquartstein stellen sich uns die Chiemgauer Alpen in den Weg, jetzt ist der Punkt erreicht, an dem wir der Tiroler Ache flussaufwärts folgen und uns an ihrem Durchbruch nach Österreich gleich zum zweiten Mal ins Nachbarland mitreißen lassen. Aber der Ausflug ist kurz, acht Kilometer später landen wir bei Reit im Winkl erneut in Bayern. Wir umfahren die Chiemgauer Alpen zuerst im Süden, stechen dann wie ein Feldherr mittendurch: Wir tangieren den Weitsee mit seinen kleineren Brüdern Mittersee und Lödensee, staunen am noch weiter östlich gelegenen Förchensee über dessen tiefgrün spiegelnde, glasklare Oberfläche und halten uns dann im weiteren Verlauf südlich von Ruhpolding und Innzell. Hinter Schneizlreuth haben wir es beinahe geschafft: Eigentlich könnte Deutschland jetzt zu Ende sein, wenn da nicht eine Ausstülpung im Grenzverlauf wäre, die den Nationalpark Berchtesgaden nach Bayern hineinholt. In diesem Winkel der Welt ging es über Jahrhunderte turbulent zu ...; mal gehörte das heute im angrenzenden Österreich liegende Salzburg zu Bayern ..., war dann wieder eigenständig ..., auch Berchtesgaden gehörte dann für einige Jahre zu Salzburg, um danach in den Besitz Frankreichs zu wechseln. Wer sich ein klares Bild der Lage am südöstlichen Ende Deutschlands verschaffen möchte, sollte sich zuerst für ein Grund-

might be amazed to see how that puddle slowly evaporates. At Marquartstein, the Chiemgau Alps stand in our way. We've now reached the point where we follow the Tiroler Ache upstream and visit our neighboring country for the second time as we break through to Austria. But the trip is short, and eight kilometers later we land back in Bavaria at Reit im Winkl. We drive south around the Chiemgau Alps, then charge through like a trooper: We touch the Weitsee with its smaller siblings Mittersee and Lödensee, marvel at the deep green crystal-clear water of the Förchensee further in the east, and continue to the south from Ruhpolding and Innzell.

After Schneizlreuth, we've almost made it: Germany could actually end now if it weren't for a bulge at the national boundary, a protrusion that includes Berchtesgaden National Park in Bavaria. This corner of the world has experienced centuries of turbulence – Salzburg in neighboring Austria was at times part of Bavaria – before it broke away again... Berchtesgaden also belonged to Salzburg for a few years ... before changing into French hands. Those who want to get a clear picture of the situation at the southeastern end of Germany should enroll in a basic course in European history. Still, all of this is not so important to comprehend today. The neighbors on both sides of the border understand each other perfectly, there is nothing more to say. Except, perhaps, that this was not always the case; for centuries people fought fiercely for the precious resource in the mountains of this area. Salt.

The word "salt", or its Celtic version "hall", is acknowledged here in many place names: Hallstätter See, Salzkammergut, Salzach, Salzburg, Hallein, Bad Reichenhall. Since time immemorial, man hit upon white gold in the mountains – and then each other. Celtic tribes, then nobility and villagers, parishes and aristocrats – even the high clergy lost all altruism when calculating possible profit margins, and invested in greed and fraud, murder and manslaughter. Out of this ground grew an entanglement of interests that contributed to the bewildering and fascinating chapters of this region's history books. There is hardly

studium europäischer Geschichte einschreiben. Wirklich wichtig für ein Begreifen des Heute ist das alles aber nicht. Die Nachbarn hüben und drüben der Grenze verstehen sich blendend, mehr ist nicht zu sagen. Außer vielleicht, dass dies nicht immer so war: Über Jahrhunderte hinweg prügelte man sich mit Feuereifer um den großen Reichtum der Berge in dieser Gegend. Salz.

Das Wort „Salz" – oder in seiner keltischen Variante „hall" – kommt hier in vielen Ortsnamen vor: Hallstätter See, Salzkammergut, Salzach, Salzburg, Hallein, Bad Reichenhall. Schon seit grauer Vorzeit schlug man erst dieses weiße Gold im Gebirge und danach einander. Keltische Stämme, dann Adelshäuser und Dörfler, Gemeinden und Herren – selbst die hohe Geistlichkeit verlor beim Kalkulieren möglicher Gewinnspannen jegliche Nächstenliebe, investierte in Gier und Betrug, Mord und Totschlag. Auch auf diesem Boden wuchs ein Interessens-Durcheinander, das zum verwirrenden und faszinierenden Gemisch der Geschichten beiträgt, die dieses Land erzählt. Man kommt kaum an irgendeinem Ort, Winkel oder Augenblick vorüber, ohne über ganze Schichten von Geschichte zu stolpern, die sich hier ansammelt wie Guano auf Pinguin-Felsen. Verwoben und ineinander verflochten, aufeinander aufbauend. Dass das Berchtesgadener Land bis hinunter zum Königssee auch noch von dramatischer Erhabenheit ist und mit seinen schroffen Gipfeln, dem rauen Wetter und mitreißender Dynamik regelrecht wagnerianischen Pathos verströmt, trägt zu seinem speziellen Charakter bei. Mit einem kräftigeren Tusch, Pauken- und Posaunendonner hätte unsere Fahrt quer durch Deutschland kaum enden können.

Über die Saalach der Alpenstraße nach, vor Hintersee dann in Richtung Berchtesgaden. Der Abstecher zum Königssee muss nicht nur für Freunde der deutschen Volksmusik sein, der Anblick des weit ins Gebirge geschnittenen Sees ist immer wieder magisch. Spiegelverkehrte Welt auf der glasklar daliegenden Wasseroberfläche, Berge kopfüber, blauer Himmel ins Wasser gefallen, Schwäne und strahlend weiße Ausflugsboote ebenso. In Berchtesgaden angelangt steht uns eine weitere Reise bevor, eine ins exakte Gegenteil von romantisch, lieblich und unbeschwert: Am Obersalzberg sammelte sich die Elite Nazi-Deutschlands rund um Adolf Hitler in einem abgeriegelten Siedlungskonglomerat für dessen Bau die eigentlichen Bewohner des kleinen Berchtesgadener Ortsteils unter Zwang und Druck vertrieben wurden. Wir fahren an der heute hier installierten „Dokumentation Obersalzberg" vorbei, im Radio läuft Patti Smith: „People have the power". Rückspultaste, dann laut mitsingen: "And my sleeping, it was broken, but my dream, it lingered near ..., the people have the power". So geht es zum Rossfeld, der mautpflichtigen Panoramastraße auf einer wahrhaften Alpenaussichtsterrasse, der letzten Straße am Ende Deutschlands. Es sind die besten Kilo-

Man kommt kaum an irgendeinem Ort, Winkel oder Augenblick vorüber, ohne über ganze Schichten von Geschichte zu stolpern, die sich hier ansammelt wie Guano auf Pinguin-Felsen. Verwoben und ineinander verflochten, aufeinander aufbauend.

There is hardly a town or corner or view where one doesn't stumble across layer upon layer of history that has accumulated here like guano on penguin rocks. Interwoven and intertwined, one building upon the other.

a town or corner or view where one doesn't stumble across layer upon layer of history that has accumulated here like guano on penguin rocks. Interwoven and intertwined, one building upon the other. Contributing to its special character is the fact that the Berchtesgadener Land district right down to the Königssee is also of full of dramatic grandeur and, with its rugged peaks, harsh weather and invigorating dynamism, exudes a Wagnerian pathos. Our journey across Germany could hardly have ended with a more booming timpani and trombone fanfare.

Following the Saalach tributary along the Alpenstraße, and before reaching Hintersee we head towards Berchtesgaden. A detour to the Königssee is not just for fans of German folk music. The sight of the lake, which cuts far into the mountains, is always magical. A world mirrored in the crystal clear water, upside-down mountains, blues skies fallen into the lake, rippled by swans and bright white pleasure boats. Arriving in Berchtesgaden there is one more discovery; one that is the antithesis of romantic, charming and carefree: At Obersalzberg, the Nazi Germany elite under Adolf Hitler gathered in a sealed-off compound. For its construction, the residents of the small Berchtesgaden district were forcibly driven out. Patti Smith sings as we drive past the "Dokumentation Obersalzberg" that has been erected there: 'People Have The Power'. We press the rewind button and sing along at the top of our voices: 'And my sleeping, it was broken, but my dream, it lingered near... people have the power.' And so it continues to Rossfeld, the scenic toll road on a truly panoramic terrace, the last road at the end of Germany. These are the best kilometers of the day and we savor each one of them – we know our trip is coming to

meter dieses Tages, und wir genießen jeden einzelnen – auch im Bewusstsein, am Ende der Reise angekommen zu sein. Nur eine Fahrt steht uns noch bevor: Im Salzbergwerk Berchtesgaden lassen wir das Auto stehen, marschieren ins kühle Dunkel der Saline. Man drückt uns einen Overall in die Hand, und dann sitzen wir bereits auf der hölzernen, von unzähligen Hintern glattpolierten Rutschbahn ins Innere des Bergs. Tief durchatmen, ein sanfter Schubs – und wir verschwinden vom Angesicht der Erde. Die Reise ist zu Ende. Der Heimweg könnte wehmütig sein. Autobahn A 8 zurück nach München und dann weiter. Aber das auf der Salinenrutsche geweckte Kind in uns hat noch einen letzten Ausflug verdient: Hans-Peter Porsches Traumwerk in Anger liegt keine 10 Kilometer hinter Bad Reichenhall. Spielzeuge, Sportwagen, Modelleisenbahnen – eine Welt in klein. Das Träumen hört niemals auf.

an end. There is just one more ride ahead of us: we leave the car in the Berchtesgaden salt mine and stride into the cool darkness of the saltworks. We are handed overalls and take a seat in the wooden chute, polished smooth by countless butts, for a slide into the innards of the mountain. A deep breath, a gentle push – and we disappear from the face of the earth.

The journey is over. The way home could be wistful. The A8 autobahn to Munich and then onwards, but the salt-water slide has awakened the child inside. Just one more trip: Hans-Peter Porsche's Traumwerk in the village of Anger is just 10 kilometers away, just beyond Bad Reichenhall. Toys, sports cars, model trains – a miniature world. Dreaming never stops.

HOTEL & RESTAURANT

KEMPINSKI HOTEL BERCHTESGADEN
HINTERECK 1
83471 BERCHTESGADEN
WWW.KEMPINSKI.COM

ROSSFELD-PANORAMASTRASSE

ROSSFELD-
PANORAMASTRASSE

MUSEUM

HANS-PETER PORSCHE TRAUMWERK
ZUM TRAUMWERK 1
83454 ANGER
WWW.TRAUMWERK.DE

TEGERNSEE BERCHTESGADEN

Am südlich der bayerischen Landeshauptstadt München gelegenen Tegernsee angekommen, haben wir uns ins Herzland Oberbayerns vorgearbeitet. Bis ans Ende der Reise stehen uns viele, variantenreiche Kilometer über die nördlichen Alpenausläufer bevor. Wir werden tiefe Täler durchfahren, entlang kalter, klarer Seen und immer wieder über majestätisch gespannte Höhenrücken fahren. Zuerst hinüber zum Schliersee, dann durchs Leitzachtal bis Bayrischzell. Hier trudeln wir auf einer herrlichen Serpentinenstrecke aufs Sudelfeld hinauf und genießen die Ausblicke in die umliegende Bergwelt, das sinnliche und gelassene Fahren. Gleich im Anschluss geht es über die Tatzelwurmstraße nach Norden, durchs Inntal und so beinahe in direkter Richtung auf den Chiemsee zu, dem sogenannten Bayerischen Meer. Ein Besuch der berühmten Klosterinseln im See kostet einen ganzen Tag, wer diese Zeit investieren kann, sollte sie sich auf jeden Fall nehmen. Danach nehmen wir in einer südlichen Umschlingung und danach Durchquerung die Chiemgauer Alpen, landen hinter Ruhpolding und Innzell im Berchtesgadener Land. Mit der Panoramastraße am Rossfeld lassen wir die letzte Etappe unserer Reise ausklingen, ein würdiger Höhepunkt.

—

When we arrived in Tegernsee to the south of the Bavarian capital Munich, we worked our way into the heartland of Upper Bavaria. Before reaching our destination, we have many, varied kilometers ahead of us in the northern foothills of the Alps. We will drive through deep valleys, along cold, clear lakes and again and again over majestic ridges. First over to Schliersee, then through Leitzachtal to Bayrischzell. Here, we meander on a glorious snaking road up the Sudelfeld and enjoy the view of the surrounding mountains and the sensual, relaxed drive. We veer north onto the Tatzelwurm road, through the Inn Valley and almost in a straight line to Chiemsee, the so-called Bavarian Sea. A visit to the famous monastery island in the lake takes a whole day – a must-do if you have the time. Afterwards, we take a southern loop and cross the Chiemgau Alps, and after Ruhpolding and Innzell we end up in Berchtesgadener Land. With the panoramic road at Rossfeld we let the last stage of our trip roll by, a worthy highlight.

210 KM • 5 STUNDEN // 131 MILES • 5 HOURS

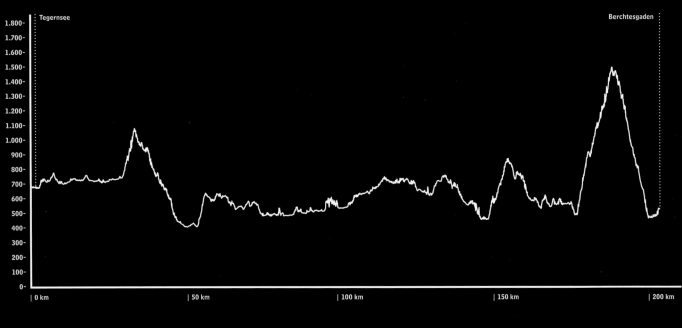

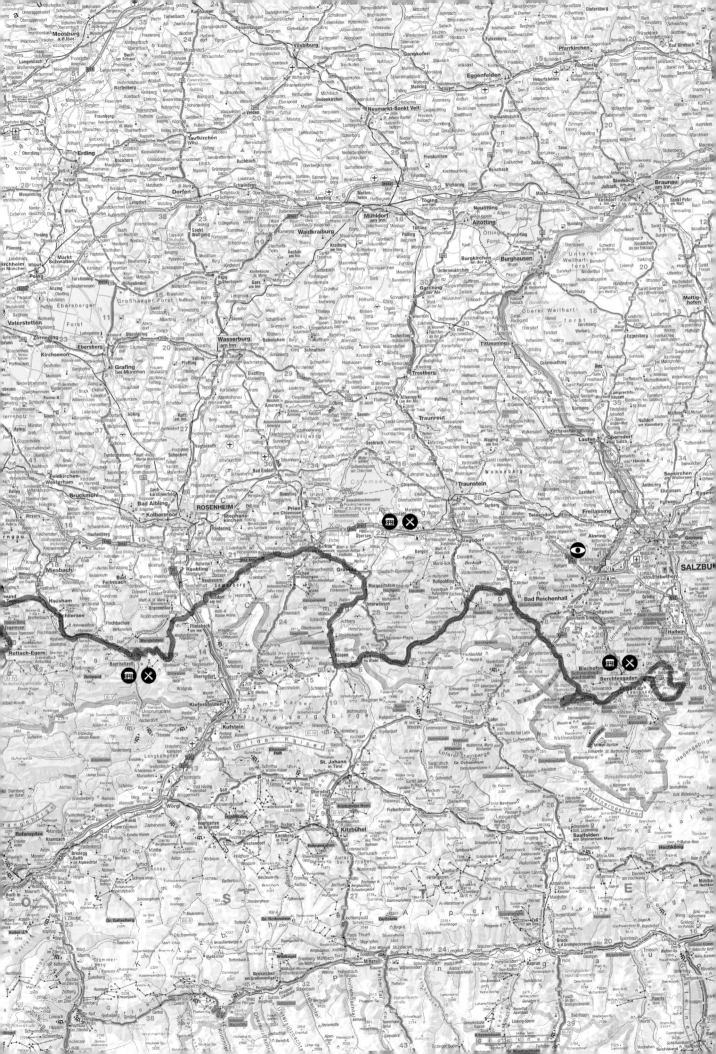

FRANZ SCHWARZ

MIKE GNANI

NIKOLAS KNOLL

MICHAEL MAUER

ASK THE LOCALS

Sie sind die Wilden aus dem Süden: Franz Schwarz führt eine Werkstatt für historischen Motorsport, ist Prototypen-Guru, Gründer des Barus-Racingteams und hat die Hände bis zu den Ellbogen in der Welt der Formel 1, der Gruppe C und des CanAm-Racing. Nikolas Knoll sucht in der ganzen Welt nach verborgenen Schätzen und Dokumenten rund um klassische Autos – sein ausgeprägter Jäger- und Sammlerinstinkt scheint dabei besonders gut auf Porsche anzuspringen. Mike Gnani ist nach Ausbildungen bei Roitmayer und Volante im Engadin als Spezialist für Porsche-Motorenbau unterwegs. Oder auf der Panamericana, in Goodwood, zwischen Peking und Paris ... Diese drei Bayern treffen auf einen Schwarzwälder: Michael Mauer prägt nach Stationen als Designer bei Mercedes-Benz und Saab seit 2004 das Design aller aktuellen Porsche-Modelle. Der Leiter der Designabteilung bei Porsche lebt den CURVES-Spirit – egal ob im Auto, beim Freeskiing oder auf dem Mountainbike.

Was heißt „zu Hause"? *FS:* Wohlfühlen. *NK:* Ruhe. *MG:* Ankommen. *MM:* Zu Hause ist dort, wo ich mich wohlfühle. Zum Wohlfühlen gehört für mich vor allen Dingen eine Umgebung, in der ich meinen Leidenschaften nachgehen kann. (Dazu braucht es vor allem Berge!)

Welcher Song ist Soundtrack deiner Hausstrecke? *FS:* „Enjoy the Silence" von Depeche Mode. *NK:* „Born to be wild". *MG:* Der Radio Edit von „Ravers Fantasy". *MM:* Motorsound.

Was ist deine Hausstrecke? *FS:* Kesselberg. *NK:* Die beginnt vor der Haustür. *MG:* Von Benediktbeuern nach St. Moritz. *MM:* Gernsbach Richtung Baden-Baden, dann Rote Lache

They are the wild men of the south: Franz Schwarz runs a workshop for historic motorsport, he is a prototype guru, the founder of the Barus Racing team and is up to his elbows in the world of Formula 1, Group C and CanAm Racing. Nikolas Knoll roams the world in search of hidden treasures and archives about classic cars – his well-honed hunter-gatherer instincts seem to be particularly targeted at Porsche cars. After training at Roitmayer and Volante in Switzerland, followed by adventures at the Panamericana, in Goodwood and between Peking and Paris, Mike Gnani has become a leading designer of Porsche engines. These three Bavarians cross paths with a man from the Black Forest: Designer Michael Mauer left Mercedes-Benz and Saab to join Porsche in 2004 and leave his indelible mark on all current Porsche models. The head of the design department at Porsche lives the CURVES spirit – in a car, freeskiing or on a mountain bike.

What does "home" mean to you? *FS:* Feeling good. *NK:* Peace. *MG:* To have arrived. *MM:* Home is wherever I feel good, and to feel good I need an environment where I can do all the things I'm passionate about – especially mountains!

Which soundtrack do you listen to on your way home? *FS:* "Enjoy the Silence" by Depeche Mode. *NK:* "Born to be wild". *MG:* The radio edit of "Ravers Fantasy". *MM:* The sound of the engine.

What is your favorite stretch of road? *FS:* Kesselberg. *NK:* It starts at the front door. *MG:* From Benediktbeuern to St. Moritz. *MM:* Gernsbach towards Baden-Baden, then the Rote Lache to Forbach... and back again on the same route.

nach Forbach. In Forbach umdrehen und die gleiche Strecke in umgekehrter Richtung.

Schrauben oder fahren? *FS:* Auto schrauben – Radl fahren. *NK:* Schrauben und fahren. *MG:* Schrauben gerne..., aber definitiv fahren! *MM:* Fahren.

Was sind die fünf besten und tollsten Autos aller Zeiten? Warum? *FS:* Bugatti 35B Grand Prix, Porsche 550, Porsche 911, Porsche Carrera GT, McLaren 675 LT – alle haben eine außergewöhnliche Technik. *NK:* Porsche 911 ST 2,3, Porsche 911 RSR 2,8, Porsche 908, Ferrari 250 SWB, Aston Martin DB4 Zagato. *MG:* Porsche 917/30: ein technisches Wunder für die 70er-Jahre, RUF Yellow Bird, Ferrari F40, Porsche Carrera GT, Lancia Delta Integrale. *MM:* Porsche 911 – besonders naheliegend, aber trotzdem objektiv ... Bugatti Type 35: Gemäß dem Motto „es ist immer schwieriger, eine Linie wegzulassen, als eine Linie hinzuzufügen" zeigt dieses Auto, was möglich ist, wenn ein Künstler wie Ettore Bugatti sich mit dem Thema Auto beschäftigt. Eine Skulptur auf Rädern, die einfach nur perfekt ist. Mercedes Pagode: Ein Auto, das mit seinen klaren Linien überzeugt und das trotz seines einzigartigen und durchaus auch polarisierenden Hardtops, von dem das Auto seinen Namen hat, extrem stimmig und harmonisch wirkt. Lamborghini Miura: einer der elegantesten Mittelmotor-Sportwagen, die es jemals gab. Vielleicht auch deshalb, weil der Miura gar keine klassischen Mittelmotor-Proportionen hat. Jaguar E-Type: klassische Proportionen „at its best" kombiniert mit sehr eigenständigen Styling-Themen, die dem Jaguar im Wettbewerbsumfeld seiner Zeit eine besondere, herausragende Position sicherten. Citroën DS: Die DS trägt ihren Zusatznamen „Die Göttin" zu Recht. Die Technik war Avantgarde, das Design war Avantgarde – und das in einer bis zu diesem Zeitpunkt nie dagewesenen Eleganz.

Was ist das Porsche-Feeling für dich? *FS:* Freiheit. *NK:* Kann ich nicht beschreiben, das muss man am Lenkradspüren. *MG:* Den ganzen Tag zwischen 6000 und 8000 Umdrehungen fahren zu können und dieses wirklich einzigartige Geräusch zu genießen. *MM:* Die perfekte Verbindung,

Do you prefer working on cars or driving them? *FS:* Working on the car – and riding a bike. *NK:* Both. *MG:* I like to work on the car... but definitely driving! *MM:* Drive.

What are the five best and most fascinating cars of all time and why? *FS:* Bugatti 35B Grand Prix, Porsche 550, Porsche 911, Porsche Carrera GT, McLaren 675 LT – they all have exceptional technology. *NK:* Porsche 911 ST 2.3, Porsche 911 RSR 2.8, Porsche 908, Ferrari 250 SWB, Aston Martin DB4 Zagato. *MG:* Porsche 917/30: a technological miracle for the seventies, RUF Yellow Bird, Ferrari F40, Porsche Carrera GT, Lancia Delta Integrale. *MM:* Porsche 911 – not surprisingly, but still objective... Bugatti Type 35: following the motto "it's always more difficult to omit a line than to add a line", this car shows what's possible when an artist like Ettore Bugatti turns his attention to cars. A sculpture on wheels that is simply perfect. Mercedes Pagode: a car that impresses with its clean lines and yet, despite its unique and polarizing hardtop, from which it gets its name, looks immensely harmonious and coherent. Lamborghini Miura: one of the most elegant mid-engine sports cars ever – perhaps also because the Miura has no classic mid-engine proportions. Jaguar E-Type: classical proportions at its best combined with very independent styling themes, which put Jaguar in an outstanding and special position in the competitive environment of its time. Citroën DS: the DS is affectionately and rightly called "The Goddess". The technology was avant-garde, the design was avantgarde – and it had an unprecedented elegance for its time.

What is the Porsche feeling for you? *FS:* Freedom. *NK:* I can't describe it. You have to feel it at the steering wheel. *MG:* To drive the whole day between 6,000 and 8,000 revs per minute and to enjoy the truly unique sound. *MM:* The perfect connection, the most intimate connection between man and machine... a driver just has to think about it and the Porsche responds. It's a directness that nourishes all senses

If there was a film about you: *FS:* "Less is More". *NK:* "The Great Enlightenment". *MG:* "Sandokan at the Limit". *MM:* None.

ie innigste Verbindung zwischen Mensch und Maschine ... in Porsche lenkt schon ein, wenn man als Fahrer nur daran enkt ... die Direktheit, mit der alle Sinne bedient werden.

Venn es einen Film über dich gäbe: *FS:* „Weniger ist mehr". *NK:* „Die große Erleuchtung". *MG:* „Sandokan at the Limit". *MM:* Keinen.

Velcher Schauspieler müsste dich spielen? *FS:* Kevin Spacey. *NK:* Peter Fonda. *MG:* Clint Eastwood. *MM:* Keine Ahnung.

Vie kommst du zu dem, was du tust? *FS:* Hobby und Interesse an der Technik. *NK:* Leidenschaft. *MG:* Aus Leidenschaft, urch den Beruf. *MM:* Die Faszination für Geschwindigkeit nd Autos und die Freude am Zeichnen.

Venn du gerade einmal nichts mit Autos zu tun hast, was nachst du dann? *FS:* Radl fahren oder Skifahren. *NK:* Jagen. *MG:* Fliegen und Zeit mit meinen Liebsten verbringen. *MM:* Skifahren oder Radfahren.

Vas ist Dein Antrieb? *FS:* Das Ergebnis. *NK:* Jagen. *MG:* Die Herausforderungen meistern! *MM:* Produkte zu getalten, die emotional berühren.

Vo liegt der Mittelpunkt der Welt? *FS:* Überall, wo es schön st, aber ziemlich genau in 6 371 300 Metern Tiefe. *NK:* In Oberbayern. *MG:* 40° 52' 0" N, 34° 34' 0" E. *MM:* In den Alpen.

Vas können die Bayern/Schwarzwälder besonders gut? Und vas überhaupt nicht? *FS:* Konsequent sein in Entscheidunen und gut leben. Sie sind wenig tolerant gegenüber Nicht-Bayern – mit Ausnahmen! *NK:* Einfach nur sein. Englisch hne Akzent. *MG:* Geradeaus/ehrlich sein. Hochdeutsch. *MM:* Gut: Wertschätzung der Natur. Überhaupt nicht: Hochdeutsch.

Velche Leibspeise aus deiner Ecke müssten die Leute auf der ganzen Welt mal essen? *FS:* Kartoffelcarpaccio mit Bergkäse und Urwaldpfeffer oder Olivenöl von Michaela. *NK:* Die bayerischen Klassiker mit ein oder zwei gut gezapften Halben. *MG:* Schnitzel mit Bratkartoffeln und Preiseleeren. *MM:* Rehrücken mit Spätzle ... das sagt ein Vegetarier.

And which actor would play you? *FS:* Kevin Spacey. *NK:* Peter Fonda. *MG:* Clint Eastwood. *MM:* No idea.

How did you end up doing what you do? *FS:* Hobby and interest in technology. *NK:* Passion. *MG:* Out of passion, through the profession. *MM:* The fascination for speed and cars and the joy of drawing.

What do you do when you're not doing car stuff? *FS:* Biking or skiing. *NK:* Hunting. *MG:* Flying and spending time with my loved ones. *MM:* Skiing or cycling.

What motivates you? *FS:* The result. *NK:* Hunting. *MG:* Mastering the challenges! *MM:* Designing products that evoke emotion.

Where is the centre of your world? *FS:* Wherever you find beauty, but actually 6,371,300 meters deep to be precise. *NK:* In Upper Bavaria. *MG:* 40° 52' 0" N, 34° 34' 0" E. *MM:* In the Alps.

What are the Bavarians/Black Foresters good at? And what are they not at all good at? *FS:* Being consequent in making decisions and living well. They're not so tolerant of non-Bavarians – with exceptions! *NK:* Just living. English without an accent. *MG:* Straight up and honest. High German. *MM:* Good: an appreciation of nature. Not good: High German.

What favorite food from your region should people from all over the world try? *FS:* Potato carpaccio with mountain cheese and Madagascar black pepper or Michaela's olive oil. *NK:* The Bavarian classics with one or two freshly-tapped pints. *MG:* Schnitzel with fried potatoes and cranberries. *MM:* Venison with spaetzle... and I'm a vegetarian.

BAC KST AGE

Es ist ein sonderbares, beinahe feierliches Gefühl, mit CURVES in Süddeutschland unterwegs zu sein. Und das hat einen ganz bestimmten Grund: Die Mannschaft hinter CURVES kommt von hier, Süddeutschland ist unsere Hausstrecke. Wir sind mit dem Duft der Wälder und Wiesen aufgewachsen, mit dem Gefühl von süßem Seewasser in den Haaren. Unsere Beine wachsen vermutlich ein klein wenig schräg, weil wir Berge gewöhnt sind, und unsere Art zu denken ist auf dem Denken der vielen Generationen vor uns gewachsen: Wir sind Bayern, wir sind Schwaben, wir sind Schwarzwälder. Auf diese CURVES-Ausgabe haben wir uns deshalb schon lange gefreut. Wir haben sie regelrecht unausweichlich kommen sehen. Vielleicht hätten wir unsere Leser ja bereits viel früher hier herumführen sollen, so schön wie wir es haben. Aber das tut man nicht, das wäre schlecht erzogen, sehr aufdringlich, und schließlich mussten wir einander auch erst einmal kennenlernen. Daher also die langen Umwege über die halbe Welt, bis wir endlich im Schwarzwald gelandet sind, in Schwaben und Bayern. Natürlich

It is a special, almost festive feeling to travel with CURVES through Southern Germany. And there's a good reason: The CURVES crew comes from here. Southern Germany is our home turf. We grew up with the tang of the forests and meadows, with the feeling of sweet lake water in our hair, with slightly uneven legs due to the undulating mountainscape – and our way of thinking, which has its roots in the many generations before us: We are Bavarians, we are Swabians, we are people of the Black Forest. And we have been looking forward to this CURVES edition for a very long time. There was just no way around it. Perhaps we should have brought our readers on this trip much earlier – it's beautiful here. But it's just not done. It would have been impolite, pushy and, we first had to get to know each other, anyway. Hence, it took long detours around half the world until we finally arrived in the Black Forest, in Swabia and Bavaria. Of course, that's only half the story. For a while, we may have doubted that anyone would be interested in this part of Germany; an area that is so familiar and often-seen for us. Why would anyone get excited about the

Wer sollte zum Bodensee fahren wollen, wenn es das Mittelmeer oder gar die Strände Thailands gibt? Weshalb Bayern, wenn es die Schweiz, Südtirol oder Schottland sein kann? – Und dann war da diese kleine, leise Stimme in uns. „Hey", sagte sie, „so geht es allen Menschen mit ihrer Heimat: Man sieht sie oft, sie wird gewöhnlich und klein. In Wirklichkeit aber ist sie unsagbar schön und spannend, mach mal die Augen auf ..." Genau das haben wir dann getan: Die Augen auf.

ist das aber nur die halbe Wahrheit. Ein kleines Stück weit haben wir vielleicht immer gezweifelt, dass sich irgendjemand für diesen Teil Deutschlands interessieren könnte, der für uns altbekannt und viel gesehen ist. Weshalb sollte man sich denn für den Schwarzwald begeistern, wenn man die Rocky Mountains oder die Pyrenäen haben kann? Wer sollte zum Bodensee fahren wollen, wenn es das Mittelmeer oder gar die Strände Thailands gibt? Weshalb Bayern, wenn es die Schweiz, Südtirol oder Schottland sein kann? – Und dann war da diese kleine, leise Stimme in uns. „Hey", sagte sie, „so geht es allen Menschen mit ihrer Heimat: Man sieht sie oft, sie wird gewöhnlich und klein. In Wirklichkeit aber ist sie unsagbar schön und spannend, mach mal die Augen auf ..." Genau das haben wir dann getan: Die Augen auf. Und auf einmal haben wir gesehen, wie tief und magisch und herrlich schwer der Schwarzwald sein kann. Wie reich und lieblich, wie lebendig und vielfältig das Allgäu und Schwaben sind. Wie majestätisch und wild, wie ehrlich, erdig und aufregend Bayern ist. Ab dann konnten wir es kaum noch erwarten, endlich loszufahren. Man möchte seine Gäste herumführen, sie begeistern und mitreißen, ihnen die Perspektive eines Einheimischen vermitteln. Weil man eben stolz auf sein Zuhause ist. Wenn dieses CURVES also vor allzu tiefen Einblicken strotzt, sehen Sie es uns nach. Wir haben keinen neutralen Zugang zu dieser Ecke der Welt, wir sind tief befangen. Vielleicht schaffen wir es trotzdem, mit diesem CURVES den Baden-Württembergern und Bayern unter unseren Lesern die Heimat neu zu erzählen. Vielleicht schaffen wir es auch, den CURVES-Lesern, die an einer weit entfernten Startlinie losgefahren sind und sich nun etwas eingeschüchtert umsehen, zu sagen: „Willkommen in unserem Garten, in unserem Wohnzimmer, unserem Kinderzimmer. Willkommen in unserer Heimat."

Wir finden, die Zeit für diese beinahe private Tour mit Freunden ist nun wirklich reif. Wo sind wir nicht schon überall zusammen gewesen, vom hohen Norden bis in den tropischen Süden, da könnte es doch nun wirklich angebracht sein, die CURVES-Leser einmal mit zu uns nach Hause zu nehmen. Schließlich ist auch das ein wesentlicher Aspekt der CURVES-Idee: Unterwegssein mit Freunden, in Gegenden, die einem das Herz öffnen. Und wo wird man denn schon so schwach

Who would want to visit Lake Constance when there is the Mediterranean or even beaches in Thailand? Why Bavaria when there is Switzerland, South Tyrol or Scotland? But then that quiet voice inside whispers: "Hey, everyone thinks like this about their own country. You're so used to it that it seems ordinary and insignificant. In reality, though, it's incredibly beautiful and enthralling, just open your eyes..."

Black Forest when they can have the Rocky Mountains or the Pyrenees? Who would want to visit Lake Constance when there is the Mediterranean or even beaches in Thailand? Why Bavaria when there is Switzerland, South Tyrol or Scotland? But then that quiet voice inside whispers: "Hey, everyone thinks like this about their own country. You're so used to it that it seems ordinary and insignificant. In reality, though, it's incredibly beautiful and enthralling, just open your eyes..."

So we did just that: Opened our eyes. And suddenly we saw how deep and magical and wonderfully weighty the Black Forest can be. How rich and charming, how lively and diverse the Allgäu and Swabia are. How majestic and wild, authentic, earthy and exciting Bavaria is. We could hardly wait to finally start our trip. One yearns to show guests around, inspire and thrill them, give them a local's perspective – because you're proud of your home. So, if this CURVES issue is overflowing with deep insights, we ask for your understanding. We are not impartial when it comes to this corner of the world, we are deeply biased. Perhaps we manage to tell even the readers from Baden-Württemberg and Bavaria the story of their home in a different way. Perhaps we can also tell the CURVES readers who set off from a distant starting line and now look around feeling a little intimidated: Welcome to our garden, our living room, our nursery. Welcome to our home.

wie zu Hause. – „Backstage", nennen wir dieses Kapitel, und da darf ganz bestimmt aus dem Nähkästchen geplaudert werden: Bei CURVES haben wir eine bekannte Schwäche für den Verlauf von Kurven, von Gelände, von Topographie. Es bereitet uns immer noch eine Gänsehaut, mit dem Helikopter oder Flugzeug über eine Landschaft aufzusteigen und dann alles aus der Vogelperspektive zu betrachten. Die unerklärliche Ästhetik von ins Gelände gegossenen Straßen zu bestaunen, die wir später mit dem Auto emotional abtasten. Als dann aber die Fotos der im Wolkendunst badenden Schwarzwaldberge vor uns lagen, die Bilder der beinahe asiatisch anmutenden Kesselberg-Strecke am Walchensee oder des endlosen, schroffen, furchteinflößenden Gebirgspanoramas rund um die Eng – da haben wir einen dicken Kloß der Rührung hinuntergeschluckt.

„Mia san mia" sagen die Bayern, „Dahoim isch's am scheenschta" die Schwaben und Nichts die Schwarzwälder. Aber das ist keineswegs so vereinnahmend, abgeschlossen und abweisend gemeint, wie es sich anhört: Wir lieben den Gedanken, all die CURVES-Leser mitzunehmen, wir wollen das alles überhaupt nicht für uns haben. Schließlich sind auch wir schon häufig mitgenommen worden, gerade auch bei der Produktion dieser CURVES-Ausgabe. Einige der Routen im Nordschwarzwald kannten wir überhaupt nicht, und es ist der zielstrebigen Pace von Porsche-Chefdesigner Michael Mauer zu verdanken, dass wir nun ein paar Routen-Kniffe mehr draufhaben. Auch Porsche-Mann Bastian Schramm hat sich mit leidenschaftlichem Gasfuß und unkonventionellen Auto-Reparaturmethoden in diesem CURVES verewigt. – Wer aufmerksam liest, dürfte die genaue Lage der „Bastian-Schramm-Gedächtnisecke" lokalisieren können. Ach, und sowieso sind wir von CURVES so langsam wirklich ungemein angetan von der hingebungsvollen Zuneigung der Porsche-Leute, bald schon werden wir vergessen haben, ob die nun CURVES-Fans sind oder wir Porsche-Fans. Es ist immer wieder schön mit euch da draußen, und Regine: Das Dessert war Liebe im Glas. Dankeschön.

Der Besuch bei Dornier in Friedrichshafen am Bodensee hat uns ebenfalls gut gefallen und unserem Faible fürs Fliegen neuen Auftrieb verpasst. Auch dafür: danke. Und danke von über den Wolken an die lieben Leute zu Hause: Wir sind wieder mal abgehoben und ihr konntet uns nur nachwinken. Unser Herz fliegt euch entgegen. Familie, Freunde – ihr seid unsere Lieblings-Bayern und Herzens-Schwarzwälder. „Pfiat di forever, sauwer bleiwe." Das Unterwegssein durch eine so bekannte Welt hat uns ganz neu daran erinnert, wie sehr es sich lohnt, jeden einzelnen Kilometer zu schätzen. Dass wir ein Gefühl von Heimat in uns tragen, kann nur bedeuten, dass es einem anderen Menschen woanders genauso geht. Zuhause, das ist überall für irgendjemand. Passen wir also aufeinander auf. Und auf die Heimat. Wo immer sie auch ist. Überall.

We think the time for this almost private tour with friends is overdue. We've been almost everywhere together, from the far north to the tropical south, so it is high time to take our CURVES readers home with us. After all, this is an essential part of the CURVES concept: being on the road with friends in regions that open the heart. And there is nowhere that makes the heart grow fonder than home. We've called this chapter "Backstage", and it's where we get to chat heart-to-heart: At CURVES, we have a well-known weak spot for snaky roads, for terrain and topography. It still gives us goosebumps to fly in a helicopter or plane and see everything from above. To admire the inexplicable aesthetics of roads carved into the land, which we will later discover emotionally by car. But when we see the photos of the Black Forest mountains bathed in the cloudy haze before us, and the images of the almost Asian-looking Kesselberg route at Lake Walchensee or the endless, rugged, fearsome mountain panoramas around the Eng – we have to swallow a big lump of emotion.

"Mia San Mia" (we are who we are), say the Bavarians. "Dahoim isch's am scheenschta" (east or west, home is best), say the Swabians. The people of the Black Forest say nothing. This is by no means as possessive, closed and dismissive as it may sound: We love the idea of taking all CURVES readers with us; we don't want to keep this to ourselves. After all, we too have often been taken by the hand – and especially in the production of this CURVES issue. Some of the routes were totally foreign to us, and it is thanks to the determined pace of Porsche's chief designer Michael Mauer that we now have a couple of new tips. Porsche man Bastian Schramm also immortalized himself in this CURVES issue with a passionate throttle foot and unconventional car repair methods – if you read carefully, you will be able to identify the exact location of the "Bastian Schramm Monument Corner". Well, anyway, we at CURVES are slowly becoming tremendously taken with the devotion of the Porsche people, and soon we'll have forgotten whether they are CURVES fans or we are Porsche fans. It's always wonderful to be out there with you, and Regine: your dessert was love in a glass. Dankeschön. We also enjoyed our visit to Dornier in Friedrichshafen at Lake Constance, which revived our passion for aviation: Thank you so much. And thanks from above the clouds to our dear ones at home: We've taken off again and you were only able to wave goodbye. Our hearts fly to you. Family, friends, you are our favorite Bavarians and Schwarzwälder. Pfiat Di (may god lead you) forever, and sauwer bleiwe (stay out of trouble).

Being on the road through such a familiar world reminded us anew of how important it is to appreciate every single kilometer. The fact that we carry a feeling of home in us can only mean that another person somewhere else feels exactly the same. Let's take care of each other. And our home. Wherever that may be. Everywhere.

Und dann war da dieser eine Tag: Zehn magische Porsche zwischen Wahnsinn und Glorie materialisieren sich auf den Straßen zwischen Schwarzwald und Karwendelgebirge. Wir durften dabei sein, mit schwachen Knien – für diese epischen Momente sagen wir Danke: Thomas im gnadenlosen, einzigartigen 918. Christophe, der nicht nur einen Carrera GT, sondern auch den 550 Spyder ins Sonnenlicht geschoben hat. Dem großartigen Malte im ebenso großartigen 906. Dem Porsche Zentrum München, die tatsächlich einen 914/6 flott machen konnten – und wie flott. Thommy, der einen donnernden 962 ins Freie gelassen hat, direkt vor unseren Augen und Ohren. Dann kam Daniel im Ex-Stirling-Moss-904 – wir stehen still und grüßen über die Welten hinweg. Ein herzhaftes Dankeschön geht auch raus an Familie Deutsch: „Einfach so" das originale „Le Mans"-Kameraauto von Steve McQueen/H. Linge rauszuholen, den famosen 908/48, das hat Format. Und last but not least: Danke ans Porsche Museum für die radikale Bergspyder-Studie und an Porsche Deutschland für den GT4, der wie ein Derwisch zwischen all den Legenden unterwegs war – und selbst eine werden wird.

And then there was this one day: ten magical Porsches between madness and glory materialize on the roads between the Black Forest and the Karwendel Mountains. We were allowed to be there, weak-kneed – for these epic moments we say thank you: Thomas in the merciless, unique 918. Christophe, who not only pushed a Carrera GT, but also the 550 Spyder into the sunlight. To the great Malte in the equally great 906. To Porsche Zentrum Munich, who could actually make a 914/6 run again - and not too bad, either. Tommy, who let a thundering 962 out into the open, right before our eyes and ears.

Then came Daniel in the ex-Stirling Moss 904 – we stand still and salute across the worlds. A heartfelt thank-you also goes out to the Deutsch family: to get the famous 908/48 out into the open "just like that", the original Steve McQueen/H. Linge camera car from "Le Mans", that's quite something. And last but not least: thanks to the Porsche Museum for the radical Bergspyder study and to Porsche Deutschland for the GT4, which was going like a dervish between all the legends – and will become one itself.

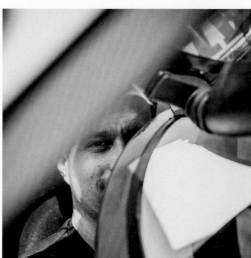

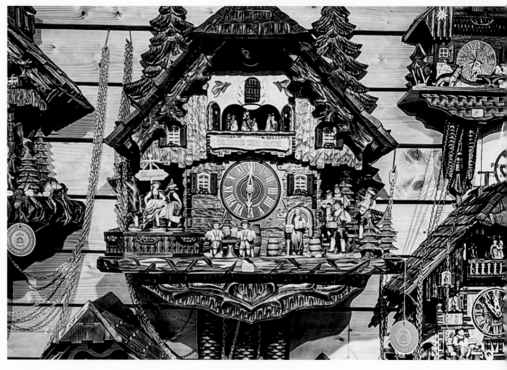

DANK AN / THANKS TO

BASTIAN SCHRAMM, MAXIMILIAN RAMISCH, SEBASTIAN FICHTER, BEN WINTER, NADJA KNEISSLER, JÖRN HEESE,
AXEL GERBER, HANNO VIENKEN, MICHAEL DORN, MICHAEL DAIMINGER, MICHAELA BOGNER, STEFAN WEYERER, MICHAEL FISCHER

SPECIAL FX / SPECIAL FX

MALTE FROMM • CHRISTOPHE SCHMID • FAMILIE DEUTSCH/DEUTSCH MECHANIK • TOMMY SCHLERET • THOMAS BECKMANN • DANIEL MAIER • MIKE GNANI
MARKUS GÜNTHER • PORSCHE MUSEUM • PZ MÜNCHEN • HANS JÖRG GÖTZ • PETER LENDLE • MARKUS KLUSKA • ANDREAS MIERSWA • FERDINAND WOLF (SKYNAMIC)
MICHAEL MAUER • FRANZ SCHWARZ • NIKOLAS KNOLL • STAATLICHES BAUAMT TRAUNSTEIN • LANDRATSAMT BERCHTESGADENER LAND

COPYRIGHT: Das Werk einschließlich aller seiner Teile ist urheberrechtlich geschützt. Jede Verwertung außerhalb der engen Grenzen des Urheberrechtsgesetzes bedarf der Zustimmung des Urhebers und des Verlags. Die im Inhalt genannten Personen und Handlungen sind frei erfunden. Sollten Ähnlichkeiten mit tatsächlich existenten Personen oder stattgefundenen Handlungen entstanden sein, oder sollte ein solcher Eindruck entstehen, so ist dies unsererseits auf keinen Fall gewollt oder beabsichtigt. Die in diesem Magazin enthaltenen Angaben wurden nach bestem Wissen erstellt. Trotzdem sind inhaltliche und sachliche Fehler nicht vollständig auszuschließen. Deshalb erfolgen alle Angaben ohne Garantie des Verlags und der Autoren. Für die Inhalte übernehmen wir keinerlei Gewähr oder Verantwortung. COPYRIGHT: All rights reserved. No part of this work may be reproduced or used in any form or by any means - without written permission from the author and the publisher. Any mentioned person and/ or actions are fictitious. Should there be any similarity to a real existing person or an action, or should such an impression could be originated, it has not been the intention by any means. All information published in this magazine have been produced to the best of one's knowledge. Nevertheless, mistakes regarding contents and objectivity cannot be eliminated completely. Therefore, all the specifications can only be published without guarantee from the publisher's and the author's side. For the contents, there will be no warranty or guarantee.

Kraftstoffverbrauch/Emissionen* Porsche 718 Cayman GT4

Kraftstoffverbrauch/ Emissionen des Porsche 718 Cayman GT4/ Fuel consumption Porsche 718 Cayman GT4
Kraftstoffverbrauch kombiniert: 10,9 l/100km, CO_2-Emissionen kombiniert: 249 g/km
Combined fuel consumption in accordance with EU 6: 718 Cayman GT4: 10,9 l/100 km, CO_2 emissions: 249 g/km

* Die angegebenen Werte wurden nach dem vorgeschriebenen Messverfahren (§ 2 Nr. 5, 6, 6a Pkw-EnVKV in der jeweils geltenden Fassung) ermittelt.
* Data determined in accordance with the measurement method specified by Section 2 No. 5, 6, 6a of the German Ordinance on the Energy Consumption Labelling of Passenger Cars (PkW-EnVKV) in the version currently applicable.

IMPRESSUM / IMPRINT

HERAUSGEBER/
PUBLISHER: CURVES MAGAZIN
THIERSCHSTRASSE 25
D-80538 MÜNCHEN

VERANTWORTLICH FÜR
DEN HERAUSGEBER/
RESPONSIBLE FOR
PUBLICATION:
STEFAN BOGNER

KONZEPT/CONCEPT:
STEFAN BOGNER
THIERSCHSTRASSE 25
D-80538 MÜNCHEN
SB@CURVES-MAGAZIN.COM

DELIUS KLASING
CORPORATE PUBLISHING
SIEKERWALL 21
D-33602 BIELEFELD

REDAKTION/
EDITORIAL CONTENT:
STEFAN BOGNER
BEN WINTER

ART DIRECTION, LAYOUT,
FOTOS/ART DIRECTION,
LAYOUT, PHOTOS:
STEFAN BOGNER

MAKING OF FOTOS:
MICHAEL DAIMINGER
MARKUS KLUSKA

TEXT/TEXT: BEN WINTER
TEXT INTRO/TEXT INTRO:
BEN WINTER

MOTIVAUSARBEITUNG
LITHOGRAPHIE/SATZ/

POST-PRODUCTION,
LITHOGRAPHY/SETTING:
MICHAEL DORN

KARTENMATERIAL/MAP
MATERIAL: MAIRDUMONT,
OSTFILDERN

ÜBERSETZUNG/TRANSLATION
KAYE MUELLER

PRODUKTIONSLEITUNG/
PRODUCTION MANAGEMENT:
AXEL GERBER/JÖRN HEESE

DRUCK/PRINT:
KUNST- UND WERBEDRUCK
BAD OEYNHAUSEN

2.AUFLAGE/2ND EDITION:
ISBN 978-3-667-12115-8

AUSGEZEICHNET MIT / AWARDED WITH

DDC GOLD - DEUTSCHER DESIGNER CLUB E.V. FÜR GUTE GESTALTUNG // IF COMMUNICATION DESIGN AWARD 2012
BEST OF CORPORATE PUBLISHING // ADC BRONZE // RED DOT BEST OF THE BEST & D&AD // NOMINIERT FÜR
DEN DEUTSCHEN DESIGNPREIS 2015 // WINNER AUTOMOTIVE BRAND CONTEST 2014 // GOOD DESIGN AWARD 2014

CURVES AUSGABEN / OTHER ISSUES OF CURVES

PYRENÄEN
PYRENEES
Im Handel erhältlich/Available in stores

ÖSTERREICH
AUSTRIA
Im Handel erhältlich/Available in stores

SCHWEIZ
SWITZERLAND
Im Handel erhältlich/Available in stores

SCHOTTLAND
SCOTLAND
Im Handel erhältlich/Available in stores

FRANKREICH
FRANCE
Im Handel erhältlich/Available in stores

USA · KALIFORNIEN
USA · CALIFORNIA
Im Handel erhältlich/Available in stores

SIZILIEN
SICILY
Im Handel erhältlich/Available in stores

NORDITALIEN
NORTHERN ITALY
Im Handel erhältlich/Available in stores

DEUTSCHLAND/DÄNE.
GERMANY/DENMARK
Im Handel erhältlich/Available in stores

SPANIEN · MALLORCA
SPAIN · MALLORCA
Im Handel erhältlich/Available in stores

USA · COLORADO/UTAH
USA · COLORADO/UTAH
Im Handel erhältlich/Available in stores

THAILAND
THAILAND
Im Handel erhältlich/Available in stores